Sick of never winning a fantasy and do something about it. In statistical analysis, graphs, illustrations, and impressively large words like "impressively," *Fantasy Football for Winners* gives you the tools to dominate your league year after year until you are too senile to care.

Learn earth-shattering solutions to brain-shattering quandaries such as:

-- Neutralizing the adverse impact of injuries
-- Executing favorably lopsided trades that appear fair
-- Keeping your family on the other side of the house on game days

Do quarterbacks perform better after a loss? How accurate are popular website player rankings? Fantasy football championships begin with diligent research, insightful analysis, and reading this book. Too busy? Too schmizzy. If you have time to poop or pick your nose, then you have time to transform your fantasy life via *Fantasy Football for Winners*— the award-winning-seeking fantasy tome that belongs on every bookshelf in America, preferably in front of other books.

So gain a permanent edge on that turd in Accounting, and start making all of your fantasies come true . . . one player at a time.

What others are saying about
Fantasy Football for Winners . . .

"B.J.'s book demonstrates a depth of insight into fantasy football that can only be achieved through long hours of analysis-- unfortunately at the expense of cultural awareness, exercise, normal human interaction, and basic personal grooming. Remind me again how this guy found a wife."

-- Andrew Birch, economist

"This book covers fantasy football better than the one I wrote about creating your own murder mystery party."

-- Joseph J. Franco, author of *How to Create Your Own Murder Mystery Party*

"If this book had been around seven years ago when I started playing fantasy sports, I would be paying MUCH less for therapy these days."

-- Josh Gaffga, musician and middle school teacher

"Just like B.J.'s book, fantasy football is a work of capitalistic art. Where else can you spend so much psychological and emotional energy for such a life-changing return?"

-- Hans Hess, CEO EnviroCab and Elevation Burger

"*Fantasy Football for Winners* is as American as mom and apple pie, where 'mom' is a stud fantasy running back and 'apple pie' is 1,800 all-purpose yards and 15 touchdowns. It's also great for long visits to the bathroom."

-- Chris Hood, car auction marketing specialist

"I used to be a sniveling wimp, finishing last every year. I was the laughingstock of my league. Since I've been practicing B.J.'s art of *kick-ass* fantasy football, my opponents now fear me."

-- Dan Johnson, psychiatrist

Fantasy Football for Winners

**The Kick-Ass Guide
to Dominating Your League
From the World's Foremost Fantasologist**

By B. J. Rudell

Illustrated by Will Harding

Extra Point Press

Extra Point Press
Austin Texas
United States
www.XPPress.com
Library of Congress Control Number: 2012935134
ISBN: 978-1-936635-11-5
Copyright © 2012 by B. J. Rudell
All rights reserved
Edited by Trish Hendricks

Visit the publisher at www.ExtraPointPress.com

Printed in the United States of America by Lightning Source

Bulk purchases, please contact
info@ExtraPointPress.com

Dedicated to the 99-yard touchdown pass

and other life-affirming fantasy moments.

Table of Contents

Introduction ix

PART I: The Offseason

Chapter 1: So You Think You've Got What It Takes 2

Chapter 2: Why Me? 7

Chapter 3: Embracing Mediocrity: a *Kick-Ass* Approach to Winning 22

Chapter 4: Introducing Dirk Hardy and Jo-Jo Mc'scuses 28

Chapter 5: Fielding/Finding a League You Can Dominate 34

PART II: The Preseason

Chapter 6: Fly Solo or Partner Up? 40

Chapter 7: Bracing Others for What's to Come 48

Chapter 8: Picking a Team Name That Doesn't Suck 55

Chapter 9: Preliminary Research 60

Chapter 10: Draft Prep 72

Chapter 11: Kicking Ass on Draft Day 95

Chapter 12: Post-Draft Research (You're Not Done Yet) 115

Chapter 13: How's My Money Doing? (Keeping Tabs on the Pot) 124

PART III: The Regular Season

Chapter 14: Roster and Lineup Decisions: Pregame Dos and Don'ts 132

Chapter 15: Watching Games the *Kick-Ass* Way 152

Chapter 16: To Take or Not to Take: That Is the Fantasy Question 159

Chapter 17: The Right Time to Cut a Player Loose   182

Chapter 18: Injuries = Opportunities   197

Chapter 19: The Rebound Effect (a.k.a. the *Kick-Ass* Law of Averages) 203

Chapter 20: Bye   219

Chapter 21: A Lost Art: Executing Uneven Trades That Seem Fair   224

Chapter 22: Those Unreliable Gut Feelings   235

Chapter 23: Offsetting the Inconvenience of Obligatory Travel   241

PART IV: The Postseason

Chapter 24: Step It Up   248

Chapter 25: Concession Speech: Jo-Jo Mc'scuses   251

Chapter 26: Victory Speech: Dirk Hardy   254

PART V: The Offseason (Redux)

Chapter 27: Victory Banquet   260

Chapter 28: Was It Worth It?   263

INTRODUCTION

"You cannot open a book without learning something."
– Confucius

Fantasy Football for Winners must not be taken too seriously. It also must be taken very seriously. Confused? So is my publisher.

What you are about to read—possibly in one sitting, but more likely in 100+ sittings between frequent bathroom breaks (go get that checked out)—is both sincere and satirical. These distinctions should be clear throughout. For example, outlining effective trade strategies is sincere, while advising you to abandon your family for fantasy fortune is satirical. See the difference? If not, then you might learn more from this book than I intended, which is troubling.

Aside from a 2009 study by the Harvard College Sports Analysis Collective on indoor/outdoor field goal kicking, all statistical findings contained in this book are mine, and I stand by their accuracy, which was earned through the painstaking collection, checking, and re-checking of all data and formulas.

For two years I devoted thousands of hours to fantasy research, analysis, and writing. Don't let it go to waste. I sincerely hope that you will adopt my unique fantasy approach—in whatever capacity time allows—and that you will dominate your league year after year. As indicated later, I wrote this book for you, the fantasy sports fan who wants to win. So go out there and kick ass. I'm rooting for you.

Many thanks to my loving and supportive wife, Carey; the rest of my comparably loving and supportive family; the gifted illustrator, Will Harding; Sam Hendricks and everyone at Extra Point Press; my frequent fantasy league competitors, from Big Kitty to Lucky Strike to Grown Ass Men to High

Top Fade; Daniel Okrent, the founder of Rotisserie League Baseball; and the thousands of professional athletes who work their asses off and give us reasons to cheer, earning their moments of professional (and fantasy) glory.

PART I

THE OFFSEASON

Famous Days in Fantasy Football History

August 28, 1968

While passing the International Amphitheatre on his way to meet friends for the fantasy football draft, Chicago native Leonard Sorensen is mistaken for an anti-war protester and arrested. From jail he uses his one allotted call to phone a draft attendee, whereupon he secures his top pick, Baltimore Colts quarterback Earl Morrall, and relays his preferred players for the next three rounds, ensuring yet another competitive team for his **Tête-à-Tête Offensives**.

It is the first of two drafts Mr. Sorensen would miss that year.

CHAPTER 1

SO YOU THINK YOU'VE GOT WHAT IT TAKES

"All types of knowledge ultimately mean self knowledge."
– Bruce Lee

You are a loser. Not the kind who picks your nose in public. Not the kind who can count all your friends on your fingers, and you have only one hand. You are the worst kind: a fantasy football loser. You compete in one or multiple leagues every year thinking *this* time will be different, that you will draft the right players and enough breaks will go your way. You have never come close to winning a championship. No team owner fears you. By Week 6 you begin scheduling other activities during games, and by Week 9 you have forgotten your league's online password, which is just as well, as you don't know how to improve your roster anyway.

Or maybe you reach the playoffs every other season and then get "screwed over" in the first round by a penalty that negates a 50-yard TD to your #1 WR, or your stud QB gets knocked out in the first quarter in the finals. You might even "strategically" determine which players to start and bench each week by catching occasional player updates on your league's website.

Which type of loser is sadder: the one who gradually stops caring, or the one who wastes several hours a week with nothing to show for it in the end? The answer, my friends, is both. You are all equally pathetic. And that is why you have purchased this book on Amazon or in some neighborhood shop that boldly defies the world's shift away from brick-and-mortar retail. That is why your parents or spouse or best-friend-who-wants-benefits bought this book for your birthday / wedding / late-in-life-Christening. Whether you *think* you are good or *know* you are bad, if fantasy titles elude you like friends on moving day, then you are a loser. Sure, you might enjoy a seemingly stellar draft, snag a couple of great free agents, and win enough games to remain hopeful until the end. Yet you still have not felt the sweet caress of victory.

If you wish to break this ugly pattern of futility, read on.

Congratulations. You are now more committed to fantasy self-improvement, having turned off the TV and made yourself more comfortable on your floor / couch / sex partner. It took a little more than one page to tear you down. In the next 250+ pages, I will rebuild you into one of the world's most fearsome fantasy weapons. So be assured: You are already well on your way to unrivaled *kick-ass* fantasy prowess.

But fantasy football success is not for everyone. I have counseled what feels like millions of people around the world, and many of them lack sufficient acumen, stamina, and independence from family and friends to triumph. If you are meek, gutless, schizophrenic, masochistic, lazy, gullible, indecisive, illiterate, easily distracted, criminally minded, an excuse maker, a hallucinator, a self-doubter, depraved, or Internet-deprived, then fantasy football is not for you, and frankly you have more pressing issues to address.

To win at fantasy football, you must make it your ultimate priority. Sports priority? No. Hobby priority? No, dammit. *Life* priority. That is what it means to be a *kick-ass* competitor. If you are 30 years old and hope to live to 80 (Health Tip #1: vitamin supplements), then fantasy football must dominate your day-to-day thinking for the next 49 years. (Health Tip #2: Devote final year of life to downing pain relievers and planning impending burial or cremation.) Whatever time you spend on sleep, match it. Whatever hours you fritter away at work, double them. Whatever moments you allocate to family, replace them.

Each week during the preseason and regular season, you must invest more than 50 hours on fantasy football. No time? Make time. Plenty of excuses? Excuse me for destroying you by 70 points. Winning requires a *kick-ass* philosophy. Stop picking daisies and start picking championship-caliber players.

Still think you've got what it takes? Read on.

In addition to dedicating yourself to fruitful fantasy conquests, you must become a perfectionist. People complain to me all the time, "But I'm not a perfectionist. I mess things up all the time, and that's okay." To which I reply, "Good-bye, fantasy loser." Harsh? No. Fair? Absolutely. You want to climb out of your loser hole? Practice absolute excellence in all fantasy activities. Stop cutting corners. Watch games with a keen eye toward not only your players, but also your opponents' roster as well as targeted free agents. Conduct research not merely to reinforce what you know, but also to widen your grasp of the fantasy landscape. Make draft picks, trades, and waiver pickups only after completing full-fledged analysis. Too much work? You disgust me. Now read on.

You must have a killer instinct; play not only to win, but to crush. Be feared in your league. Think about that for a moment . . . and smile. Picture the next time your buddy Jimmy, the aspiring astronaut, faces your team. He spends all week desperately trying to swap his QB and #2 RB knowing he has no chance of beating you without serious upgrades. Imagine your delight when everyone rejects his entreaties, leaving him sweating on Sunday morning as the day's first kickoff approaches. Fame and glory begin with making others feel incompetent and inglorious.

You must have superior at-home Internet capabilities. This is the wrong time to save for your family's birthday presents. Don't be the guy who drives to the office just to access his league account. That being said, make sure you have full access to sports information on your work computer. If your company's IT department blocks such websites, then quit. If you own the company, sell it for whatever price you can get and find a more fantasy-friendly job (or order IT to change the policy—whichever is easier).

Finally, you must be good with numbers. If multiplication tables frighten you, hire a math nerd or take a statistics class at your local college. So much of fantasy sports hinges on your ability to crunch numbers and analyze data quickly and accurately. Calculators still serve a purpose, while Excel spreadsheets might become your best friend. Although numbers should not dictate all decisions (as you will learn later), a healthy understanding will separate you from the pack. But if you come unprepared and your opponents are from math-genius countries like Germany or Singapore, save yourself the embarrassment and join a different league.

The beauty and ugliness of fantasy sports is that success is absolute. If you win, no one can take that away from you. If you lose, learn from it and move on. While you cannot change the past, you can influence the future more than you realize.

In the following chapters, you will learn my proven method for ensuring victory. It is a *kick-ass* approach that requires your full attention and comprehensive implementation. By page 37 you might say, "Oh, I've read enough to understand what this guy's talking about." You would be wrong. Each word in this book has been painstakingly written *with you in mind.* That's right: I wrote this for *you.* Understanding only half or two-thirds of my method will guarantee you only half or two-thirds success. So don't piss me off. Read the whole damn thing. That also goes for you, guy who likes to skim through books to "get the gist of it." You are pathetic. How can you devote 50+ hours per week to fantasy football when you cannot set aside 10 hours to read enlightenment in paperback form— something that will completely transform your life (and help me land a long-term book deal)?

Since the beginning of time there have been winners and losers. It is time to choose sides.

CHAPTER 2

WHY ME?

"At home I am a nice guy: but I don't want the world to know.
Humble people, I've found, don't get very far."
– Muhammad Ali

My ascension to *"kick-ass* fantasologist" was long and bumpy. Then again, I don't know anyone who has attained this status on the first try. It takes hard work, discipline, and enough experience to avoid repeating mistakes.

Football

The first NFL game I remember was Super Bowl XV in 1981, when I was seven years old. Some friends and I had a contest to see who could come closest to predicting the final score. In hindsight, it makes total sense that my first NFL memory is of a game on which I had something riding.

After learning about NFL point spreads (e.g. Denver +3 at Seattle) in 1985, I started picking which teams would cover the spread each week. Of course, that meant I had to watch. On fall Sundays at 12:55 p.m. EST (Eastern Standard Time), I parked myself on the floor of the family room, where I remained virtually motionless until the day's final contest ended. (There was no Sunday night game back then, so unfortunately this ritual lasted only about six hours).

Despite feeling enormous anxiety, brought on by a competitiveness cultivated by an older brother who absolutely despised losing and who beat me at everything, these afternoons were the most tranquil and gratifying of my childhood. Nothing compared to the anticipation felt five minutes before kickoff. And nothing compared to the exhilaration of making accurate predictions. The tightrope walk between agony and ecstasy, based on an unyielding pursuit of perfection, remains etched in my psyche to this day.

What was I betting on? Nothing at first. I played against myself, charting my progress during this first season and knowing that I would try to beat that mark the following season, and the season after that, and so on. Then my father invited me to join his work league, where we put in a few bucks (as I recall, he covered my tab, though I don't recall ever paying him back), and the weekly and season winners received year-end payouts. The pressure of playing against other people was a whole different ballgame. I was now being judged not by my own criteria of success, but by where I placed in the weekly and season-long standings. The stakes were higher. Sure, winning money would be great. But pride in knowing that I was the best among a group of 20-30 people would be much more important. I was average on athletic fields, in the classroom, and in almost every other way kids could be judged. I wanted to be the best at something. However, it was not yet my time.

I went 7-7 in my first week betting on point spreads in 1985; in other words, in half of the games I accurately predicted which team would cover the spread, and in the other half my picks were wrong. After skipping Week 2 (perhaps we took a family trip that weekend, and I had not yet learned the art of planning ahead; see Chapter 23), I finished 11-2 (11 correct picks, two incorrect picks) and 10-4 in weeks 3 and 4, respectively, bringing my season record to 28-13, which is pretty damn good—or rather, *very* damn good. Nearly anyone who has bet on point spreads would claim that a 50% mark is adequate, 55% is good, and 60% is great. I was sitting pretty at 68% without fully understanding what that meant. If I could have maintained that consistency, I could have bottled and sold it to the world—or at least to my brother.

But initiating excellence is far easier than sustaining it. I quickly fell back to Earth and finished the season at 110-and-99 (a 52.6% mark). The following year I finished with a 51.1% mark. Then 51.0%, 51.6%, and 51.7%: remarkably consistent, due entirely to a less-than-remarkable practice of following the same approach to picking the spreads without feeling compelled to improve it.

By this time I was a mainstay in my father's work league and wallowing in the middle of the standings. In 1990, my last season before leaving for college, I netted a career low mark of 49.6%; in other words, my picks against the spread were wrong more often than right. While I had taken some risks during those weeks, these decisions grew not from acquired knowledge, but from desperately trying to differentiate my predictions from the competition, as that appeared to be the only way to climb up the leaderboard. I was now officially *bad* at betting on point spreads. How did my teen years start out so promising and end so dismally?

The answer is simple, applies directly to fantasy football, and is this book's first *kick-ass* rule:

Kick-Ass Rule #1

Learn from your mistakes and *your successes. Focus on why certain decisions lead to bad results while other decisions lead to good ones. Then employ discipline to apply what you have learned.*

Once in college, I took a four-year break from betting on football spreads. But during this time I became a little more patient, a little more analytical, and a lot more competitive. When I returned to my father's office pool my first year out of college in 1995, I approached the point spread picking process with far more thoughtfulness than before and a deeper desire to win. I examined the teams, their respective trends (winning versus losing), injuries, home field advantage, and other criteria that made sense. I no longer picked purely from instinct—the dreaded "gut feelings" that are the scourge of fantasy managers everywhere (see Chapter 22). Whenever my evolving tactics led to good results, I incorporated them into my selections the following week. Whenever they led to bad results, the practice was refined or dropped. Finally, I was *learning*. Maybe I was too hasty in drawing conclusions over what worked and what did not, but my game plan was now more logical and was supportable by concrete evidence.

I finished that season at 53.2%, which to a layperson is not much better than my 52.6% performance a decade earlier. But it was my best career mark, completely reversing the downward trend of my pre-college years. And for the first time, I understood *why* it was better: I had adopted a methodical approach required to achieve success. Also consider that during my first season, I picked a majority of the games correctly in six out of 15 weeks (40%). For the five seasons that followed, that percentage ranged between 29% and 44%. However, in 1995 I picked a majority of games correctly in 10 out of 17 weeks (59%):

Picking Against the Spread

	1985	1986	1987	1988	1989	1990	1995
Number of Weeks	15	16	15	16	15	17	17
Weeks Over 50% Correct	6	7	5	6	6	5	10
% Weeks Over 50% Correct	40%	44%	33%	38%	40%	29%	59%

In its simplest terms, this means I was more consistently good in 1995 than in any previous year. It was not a matter of coasting after getting a few lucky weeks under my belt, like I had (and squandered) in 1985. Week after week I developed, implemented, and refined an approach that, objectively, yielded more success more often than ever before. I stopped picking against the spread after that season, but not before learning my first *kick-ass* rule.

Pre-Fantasy Sports

Let's rewind to 1981. At the age of eight, I created a baseball game requiring only two dice, a pad of paper, and a pencil. Each at-bat's outcome was determined by a dice roll: a three was a home run, a seven was an out, and so on. I sat on the floor and played for hours by myself, matching real MLB teams against each other in round-robin competition. Playing was akin to watching a 15-minute, nine-inning game in my mind. After each contest, I updated each team's win/loss record on a piece of paper, adjusted the divisional standings, and picked two new teams to compete. This repetitive and seemingly mindless hobby deepened my appreciation for numbers and statistics and helped me learn how to maintain singular focus for entire afternoons.

My first foray into fantasy-like sports occurred when a few friends in junior high school dragged me into a Strat-O-Matic baseball league. The game was simple and addictive for someone like me who desperately wanted to win at everything, but who almost never did. (The closest I had come at that point was reaching the finals of a 10-school sixth grade dance contest. And in case you are wondering, my moves were raw and powerful.) Each of us "drafted" players whose stats and potential turn-by-turn outcomes (single, home run, fly out, etc.) were etched across individual cards. Dice rolls determined what happened in each at-bat. Back then if your pitching staff consisted of Roger Clemens, Doc Gooden, or Mike Scott, and your lineup included either Kirby Puckett or Don Mattingly, then you had a leg up on most of the competition. Strat-O-Matic baseball seemingly had everything: drafting players, setting lineups, and the luck of the dice. Questions arose, such as:

- Whom do I draft first: a power hitter, contact hitter, starting pitcher, or relief pitcher?
- Which fielding positions yield players with the most value overall?
- In later rounds, in which positions am I weakest?
- After the draft, which player do I wish I had drafted, and what trade offer should I make to acquire him?

The strategic possibilities and potential outcomes seemed endless. I could have played for eons. And yet, after a couple of weeks, my friends grew tired of it and quit.

The following year these same friends invited me to join their new computerized baseball league. This game used a floppy disk and incorporated the same statistics used by Strat-O-Matic, but in a much more sophisticated fashion. Instead of dice, the computer program calculated the odds of each potential outcome and then—through a visual simulation—showed each pitch and result on the screen. In addition, each manager chose one of several options before each pitch to influence the pitch type (fastball, curveball, pitchout, etc.) or swing type (power, bunt, hit-and-run, etc.).

As with Strat-O-Matic, we drafted teams and met during study halls and after school to play out our season. I was immediately hooked, not just because of my success (I drafted the best team and won nine out of my first 12 games to lead the league), but also because of the game's realism. It was the closest thing I had found to managing a real team, and I wanted to play it all day, every day.

But after those first 12 games, the league folded. Why? Because the guy who ran it had a bad team. Adding insult to injury, he never returned our entry fees.

Rotisserie Sports: Fantasy's Older Brother

Today's multibillion dollar fantasy sports industry has its roots around the middle of the 20th century. But its widespread appeal took off with Rotisserie League Baseball, which started in my hometown of New York City in 1980. Less than a decade later, and probably less than a couple of miles from the game's inception, my same group of unreliable friends invited me to compete in yet another baseball competition: a Rotisserie MLB season, in which each manager collected points based on his ranking in categories such as batting average, home runs, earned run average, and saves. I partnered with my friend Tom, whose knowledge and passion for sports rivaled my own. Draft participants gathered in our school cafeteria, where we picked players at each position just as we had done in the two previous leagues. But Rotisserie was different: Instead of basing performance on past statistics, it was based on *future* statistics.

Huh? How was that possible?

Today this distinction seems elementary. In 1989 it was mind-blowing. One might draft a team of All-Stars who, due to injury, age, or other limitations, might perform significantly *below* expectations. Another might draft a team of unknowns who, due to motivation, untapped potential, and unanticipated opportunities, might perform significantly *above* expectations. Tom and I should have considered not only the previous season's statistics, but also performance trend lines, projected playing time, and other criteria to predict how each player would perform in 1989. Of course, we were high school kids with neither the time nor interest in conducting research. Additionally, we lacked the resources, as there was no Internet back then and little means of learning about any athlete beyond those playing for our hometown Yankees and Mets.

The only player I remember on our team was the Houston Astros' Bill Doran. I convinced Tom that we should draft Doran as our second baseman because he was still in his prime (30 years old), had some pop in his bat (rare for guys at his position in the '80s), and stole bases (between 17 and 42 in each of the previous five years).

Each morning we scoured the *Daily News* or *New York Post* sports section to read how our players fared the day before. Each week, one of the newspapers printed each player's season statistics across several of its pages. Dave, our friend running the league, wrote down each rostered player's stats, tabulated the  totals, and distributed the league standings to team owners every Monday. It was a drawn out, highly anticipatory process, and it was by far the most exciting game I had ever played. It sure beat rolling dice, and it increased my competitiveness (if that was possible), which heightened as the season progressed.

When summer vacation started in June, the league trudged on. But Dave was unable to tabulate stats and provide updates until we returned in September. So for three months Tom and I did not keep tabs on our players, and we were oblivious to the league standings. In hindsight we could have learned who was on each team, calculated their statistics in each category, and figured out how close to first place we were. But that would have required too much effort; I was still a relatively passive player, not having grasped the value of doing whatever it took to win. And that leads to another *kick-ass* rule:

Kick-Ass Rule #2

Be an active participant in your own success. Luck will get you only so far. Passive managers permit outcomes to be dictated for them. Active managers generate favorable outcomes by doing whatever it takes (within the rules) to win.

When we returned to school that fall, Tom approached me, exasperated: "Bill Doran is in one of the worst slumps in history!" And the situation did not improve thereafter. From June 26 through the end of the season, our second baseman batted 31-for-221 (.140 batting average). We did not win the league title. In hindsight, it was not Doran's fault. It was our fault for sitting on our asses.

Online Fantasy Sports

Out of college and out on my own, I fell in with a new group of friends that loved sports as much as I did. With the Internet taking shape as a transcendent professional sports resource, they invited me to participate in an online fantasy baseball league in 1996. I also joined a separate league with some college friends. At the beginning of the decade, I could not have imagined how fantasy sports would have evolved in only a few years. Team standings automatically updated *daily*. We could follow any player's pitches or at-bats *in real time.* All that was required was an AOL or Mindspring account, a phone hook-up, and a Pentium 75 computer that fit snugly under two-thirds of my desk.

I instantly immersed myself in all of the statistical possibilities and outcomes of my players, free agents, other owners' players, and even minor leaguers who might earn a September call-up. Although online fantasy player news was scarce, I had found a centralized news site with links to hundreds of newspaper sites, granting me easy access to the many hometown sports sections that covered my players' teams. And of course, we all still used sports magazines to supplement our budding fantasy knowledge.

In the late '90s I dabbled in fantasy basketball. After two years of NBA competition, I convinced my friends to switch to NCAA Men's Basketball—a critical lesson from which you will learn in Chapter 14.

Based on my decent success rate, I now knew I was good at fantasy sports competition, but wanted to know just how good. Emasculating a dozen guys was not satisfying enough. Oh, I still loved the competition. But I wanted to test, in a much larger arena, the skills I had learned within the safe confines of friendly leagues. So in March 2003, with MLB's spring training in full bloom, while sitting in my office cubicle, I decided to search the Web for an online league with a more global community of competitors, a clear set of rules, and a platform that encouraged *paying attention.*

Let's pause for a moment on these last two words. What does it mean to "pay attention"? As youngsters we whispered to friends in the classroom or fidgeted in church. We daydreamed while our parents told us about their boring days of youth. "Paying attention" meant exchanging fun for tedium, and that mindset is hard to shake over time. As adults, we pay attention to things that matter most:

(1) Family
   a. Remembering names, birthdays, Mother's Day, and our anniversary
   b. Half-heartedly listening to their problems
   c. Checking scores on our iPhone while stuck at the opera
(2) Money
   a. Remembering to pay our creditors each month
   b. Mentally noting where we put our wallet
   c. Making sure our bookie's odds are comparable to the odds in Vegas
(3) Health
   a. Recognizing increasing pain in joints and/or body cavities
   b. Being mindful of the risks of disfigurement
   c. Drinking only *light* beer at the ballpark
(4) Sex
   a. Interpreting her flirtatious cues
   b. Getting the damn condom on
   c. Finishing quickly so we can get back to watching the game

Armed with know-how and a competitive spirit, and with the understanding that sports was the only thing I could pay attention to in blocks longer than five minutes, I signed up for the *SportingNews* online "Baseball Basic Season 1" fantasy league, which ran from Opening Day until the All-Star break. Each owner had $30 million of fake money to spend on 10 players, each of whom was assigned a monetary value based on anticipated performance. A team was comprised of three pitchers, a catcher, a corner infielder (first or third baseman), a middle infielder (second baseman or shortstop), three outfielders, and a utility player (any hitter). Each owner was permitted a maximum number of "trades," which essentially entailed dropping a player from his team and picking up any other player he did not currently own. Each player's daily value fluctuated based on owners' transactional behavior: increased selling of a player lowered his value, while increased buying of a player increased his value.

Now let's go to the mail bag for a question:

Dear Sir/Madam,

I'm what you call a "self-starter, non-finisher": I've undertaken a lot of projects that I eventually abandoned, like horseback riding, stamp collecting, and raising my two boys. Before signing up, did you have any doubts about finishing the SportingNews *league?*

Sincerely,

Bruno F.
Tampa, Florida

Thanks for your question, Bruno. Before taking this fantasy leap, I knew what I was getting into. The rules were complex enough to make it interesting, yet simple enough to master. First I adopted a plan for the weeks leading up to Opening Day, identifying all of the factors that would contribute to fantasy success (such as researching players, anticipating player value fluctuations, and quantifying schedule impacts). Then I studied the hell out of these factors, assembling the optimal lineup to start the season, as well as instituting daily/nightly routines for ensuring continued optimal performance. My research led to several major breakthroughs—nearly imperceptible discoveries that granted me a competitive advantage over my opponents.

Success required accurately forecasting a large majority of player-by-player statistical outcomes in each of 1,200-1,300 pre-All Star break games, applying this knowledge toward buying/selling players at the right time, increasing team value to maximize buying power for high-performing players, and conserving trades. Some strategies ran counter to others, requiring me to determine when to apply one, and then when to drop it in favor of another strategy.

In this way fantasy baseball was like a puzzle. But unlike generic mathematical equations or word problems, the solution was borne out by the uncontrollable actions of hundreds of MLB players, dozens of managers and coaches, and occasional inclement weather (e.g. rainouts or midge attacks).

And this brings us to another core point:

Kick-Ass **Rule #3**

There is no concrete path to fantasy victory. Even if you think you have found the perfect strategy for your perfect team, it may need to change at any minute of any day to reflect new external information.

More than 325,000 people competed in the "Baseball Basic Season 1" *SportingNews* league. I finished in first place, netting me the $1,000 grand prize. And yes, the IRS knows about it.

The money was nice. I was living month to month and suddenly had my biggest cushion in some time. But winning meant more than the money. If this sounds strange to you, then you are a greedy bastard. And there is nothing wrong with that. But I had won despite being pulled in many other directions, including working at a full-time job and writing/editing my first book. My life was no less hectic in the years that followed, when I continued to apply and refine my *kick-ass* techniques in other *SportingNews* contests by expanding my reach to football and even venturing a couple of times into hockey. The key discovery was that my fantasy sports tactics worked. They were by no means flawless; they never are, for anyone. Yet my ensuing global rankings suggested that I was learning how to master the system with some regularity.

In total, I have finished in the top 0.11% in nine out of 16 worldwide competitions—including two first place finishes against nearly 400,000 people combined. So if you are on the toilet right now thinking, "I don't have time to do what *this* guy did," then you don't have a *kick-ass* mindset. And that is okay, because this is only Chapter 2—unless this is your third time through the book, in which case you are hopeless, but not so hopeless that you should not buy 10 more copies for your grandkids. Don't have any? Make some.

On the subject of making time, my friend Chris recently imparted these words of wisdom:

> *I've begun saying, "I don't make time" for*
> *something instead of, "I don't have time."*
> *This mindset puts me in control of my time,*
> *rather than letting time control me.*

Such *kick-ass* words have rarely been uttered by someone other than me. While just starting to date my future wife, I was busy engineering a first place finish (and $3,000 grand prize) out of 60,000+ people in the "2008 Fantasy Baseball Challenge Season 1." Yes, lonely readers, you can kick ass in fantasy *and* in romance.

So get the edge on that turd in Accounting, or on your cocky uncle who thinks he should be a GM. If you "have time" to wipe your ass, pick your nose, or scan the Internet for Rogaine sales, then you can "make time" to win your fantasy sports league. I will never say it is easy (because it never is). But anyone who is willing to make time can become a fantasy sports legend. Even you.

CHAPTER 3

EMBRACING MEDIOCRITY:

A *KICK-ASS* APPROACH TO WINNING

"What's right isn't always popular. What's popular isn't always right."
– Howard Cosell

I mentioned Bill Doran in the previous chapter not only because he is the only player I can recall having on my first fantasy sports team. He also personifies our fourth and final fundamental *kick-ass* rule:

Kick-Ass Rule #4

Mediocre players are the difference makers. Some have the potential to play like stars, either throughout the season or as week-by-week spot starters. Your fantasy success hinges largely on your ability to identify and correctly utilize these performers.

The Bill Dorans of the world can be found in every sport. These competitors are neither the best nor the worst at their position. They are just good enough to be considered in the final rounds on draft day or for your regular season starting lineup, yet are too unreliable to consistently draw attention from other owners.

In football, one example I have mentioned frequently over the years is QB Chad Pennington. With a career 90 passer rating, he was no slouch. In seasons when he was a full-time starter, his average passer rating was even higher. But aside from a brilliant 2002 campaign, in the leagues where I have played—and in friends' leagues that I have followed from afar—Pennington was never a primary option. Why not? Because too many QBs scored more fantasy points season after season. Before concluding that guys like Pennington are not worth our attention, let's take a closer look at the numbers, examining the four seasons (2002, 2004, 2006, and 2008) when he played at least 13 games.

For consistency purposes, we will begin using a standard scoring system that might not align exactly with your league's scoring rules, but which will give us a basis for accurate future comparisons: one point per 40 passing yards, one point per 10 rushing yards, one point per 10 receiving yards, six points per TD, minus two points per offensive turnover, two points per defensive turnover, one point per extra point, minus three points per missed extra point, two points per two-point conversion, one point per 50+ yard passing TD, one point per 35+ yard rushing TD, and so on.

- 2002 – 7th highest QB fantasy scorer
  - Three games with at least three TDs (a 10-TD-to-one-TO ratio in those games)
  - Three other games with two TDs and at least 200 passing yards (six TDs and two TOs total)
- 2004 – 16th highest QB fantasy scorer
  - Two games with at least three TDs (six TDs and zero TOs total)
  - Two other games with two TDs and at least 200 passing yards (four TDs and one TO total)
- 2006 – 17th highest QB fantasy scorer
  - Three games with two TDs and at least 200 passing yards (six TDs and four TOs total)
- 2008 – 11th highest QB fantasy scorer
  - Two games with at least three TDs (seven TDs and two TOs total)

▫ Three other games with two TDs and at least 200 passing yards (six TDs and three TOs total)

Pennington played 60 games during the four years when he essentially was a full-time starter. In 18 (30%) of those games, he would have been a terrific replacement for your bye week / injury-plagued / underperforming starting QB. Now let's remove 2002 from the equation, counting only the three seasons when he finished outside the top 10 at his position (while playing at least 13 games). In 12 of those 45 games (26.7%), he would have helped your club significantly. So even when discounting his best campaign, Pennington still would have helped your fantasy team at nearly the same clip, handing your team about 15-20 fantasy points a hair more than once every four contests.

And so adding Pennington to your starting lineup at the right time during his otherwise mediocre statistical seasons would have been comparable to starting a premier QB throughout the season. Therefore, if you were not fortunate enough to have landed the #1 scoring QB, starting a relatively mediocre QB like Pennington at the right time would have helped level the playing field and increased your likelihood of winning.

To all of you gentlemen and ladies and gentlemen who want to be ladies, this is a breakthrough! It is not just about Pennington, after all. There are many players like him at every fantasy position—occasional fantasy studs serving as perennial backup fantasy options. Brandon Jacobs had the 30th most RB fantasy points in 2009. In six games he finished with at least nine fantasy points, averaging just over 12 points per game in these contests. The 15th best RB, Fred Jackson, also had at least nine points in six games, though he averaged nearly four points more than Jacobs in these contests. Not surprising for a much higher ranked RB, right? However,

Jacobs outscored Jackson *seven times* (weeks 3, 4, 5, 7, 8, 11, and 13) and also performed better during Jackson's bye week than Jackson did during Jacobs' bye week. You would not know it from the final numbers, but replacing Jackson with Jacobs in 2009 would have helped your team nearly 50% of the time.

Steve Johnson established himself as a top-flight WR in 2010, finishing with the 10th most fantasy points at his position. He had at least eight points in eight different weeks. Nate Washington, on the other hand, tied for 40th in WR fantasy points, barely registering interest in all but the deepest fantasy leagues. On seven occasions he finished a game with at least eight fantasy points. Although his average output in these contests obviously was below Johnson's, Washington outscored Johnson in five weeks and tied him in another week. Would you have preferred owning Johnson that season? Absolutely. Should you have researched which opportunities to add and activate a waiver regular like Washington, thereby getting even more production for your team? Again, absolutely. Are you picking this up yet?

Fast forward to 2011. Perennial top 10 TE Jason Witten was the fifth highest fantasy scorer at his position. Ed Dickson, on the other hand, finished in 19th place. But Dickson outscored Witten five times and tied him twice. To be clear, if you started Dickson over Witten seven random times in 2011, you should not have expected him to play comparably or better every time. But—and this is vitally important—if you applied logic to predict *which games to start him and which games to sit him*, then you would have had a distinct advantage over your Aunt Martha, Cousin Fred, and everyone else who were long overdue for fantasy beat-downs. By adopting my *kick-ass* approach to disciplined investigation, you will soon learn when a *mediocre* player is more likely to shine.

If you still don't believe me, choose any free agent that performed half-decently in your league last season, such as the 30th ranked RB, 40th ranked WR, or 15th ranked DST (defense/special teams). I assure you that each of them—castoffs in most leagues—would have helped your team during several weeks of the season, sometimes outperforming even elite talent during those games.

Mediocre players are the difference-makers. They separate champions from also-rans. Everyone in your league will have a superstar or two or three. But with your pick of mediocre free agents each week, and armed with my proven, almost copyrighted techniques, you will thrive in fantasy football. Hear that, floundering line cook? Understand, washed up Olympic swimmer? Need more clues, underemployed detective?

I will write this in bold so that you will never forget it: **Your fantasy greatness hinges largely on your ability to identify which mediocre players will finish in the top 10 at their position each week.** This approach has contributed to my first place finishes over hundreds of thousands of online competitors, as well as scores of fantasy league victories among friends and co-workers. In a world where everyone is clamoring for the next best player on the draft board or angling for the top statistical performers on each week's free agent list, my *kick-ass* fantasy approach outperforms them all. It is the only proven method that is achievable year after year regardless of how successful your draft is or how many injuries jar your team.

A word of caution to you speed-readers who proudly retain only 20% of all written content: I do not condone starting only mediocre players each week. One of my former blog readers made that mistake and e-mailed me to complain. I advised him to get clean, stay in school, and stop bastardizing a system he clearly was too lazy to follow.

Nor am I suggesting that selecting mediocre players amounts to little more than guessing. I have repeatedly observed people choosing the worst player among several options. Why do they do it? They term these decisions as "educated guesses." There is nothing educated about it, and it does not lead to championships.

Too many people seek easy answers rather than put in the work required for victory. You have been warned: Follow my battle-tested path to success, or else. This journey requires intelligence, diligence, and perseverance (my three favorite "nce's"). Is my system guaranteed? Almost. Nothing in life is certain. But I am so confident you will win your league after reading the following chapters that if you fall short, simply return this book so that someone else can use it correctly.

CHAPTER 4

INTRODUCING DIRK HARDY
AND JO-JO MC'SCUSES

"The man who views the world at 50 the same as he did at 20
has wasted 30 years of his life."
– Muhammad Ali

Most fantasy leagues include a guy who has never won a championship and never will. He is not completely worthless—winning his share of regular season contests, and even making the playoffs now and then. But his flawed approach essentially ensures futility when it matters most.

Let's call him Jo-Jo Mc'scuses, and for the remainder of this book, he will be your guide. No, not the Sherpa who helps you scale the mighty Mount Everest; Jo-Jo is the guy who gets stuck inside the McDonald's bathroom at Base Camp.

I've met many Jo-Jos over the years. They are nice enough people of ordinary height and build, moderate education, and average financial means. They love their mothers, don't know their fathers very well, and were picked on as children far more than they recall. Most have an irregularly shaped head whose crown is mostly covered by carefully parted strings of unconditioned hair. And it is not uncommon to find a dark mole on one of their buttocks.

If you are lucky enough to meet one, they make the ideal fantasy league competitors (aside from the comatose). The reason, as you will see, is that Jo-Jo never works as hard as he should. His draft preparation consists of perusing another guy's outdated fantasy magazine before his turn to pick. He views players' previous seasons as the best barometers for future success, with no regard for injuries, coaching changes, personnel changes, strength of schedule, depth chart reconfigurations, or any other factor that he naively considers "negligibly pertinent." His weekly lineup decisions are rushed and irrational, derived from gut instinct and wishful thinking rather than researched evidence.

Jo-Jo is prone to making the wrong moves at the wrong times. He sticks with bad players for too long, picks up one-hit wonders a week too late, and never fails to remind other league owners, " I would've won this week if only. . ." Sadly, Jo-Jo really thinks he can be the best, but his restrictive strategy fosters eternal mediocrity—a far cry from a *kick-ass* player who, as we learned earlier, wins by capitalizing on mediocre players' best performances.

Speaking of *kick-ass* players, their role model is Dirk Hardy. You can learn everything you need to know from Dirk, and you will. He studies, analyzes, and observes from early each morning until late each night. When staring at you, he identifies your greatest weakness, to be used against you at some indeterminate time. He is an elusive creature, rarely seen at large social functions like weddings or interventions. And he is as adept at using an Excel spreadsheet as he is at using a condom with his ovulating on-again/off-again girlfriend.

Dirk approaches each fantasy season dutifully, methodically—even reverentially. He examines each player with objectivity and acumen, leading to lineup configurations that (a) maximize the probability of winning that week while (b) not leaving him vulnerable in future weeks. With such highly sophisticated and seamlessly blended short- and long-term views, Dirk's decisions are made with the precision and care of those who construct model boats in glass bottles. But unlike the bottled boats, fantasy victory cannot be broken by an enraged off-again girlfriend.

    We are now lucky enough to be joined by both Dirk and Jo-Jo:

Me: *"Dirk, it's an honor to have you here."*

Dirk: *"I accept your adulation."*

Me: *"Can you say that a little louder, so that some of our more easily distracted readers can soak it in?"*

Dirk: *"It would fall on deaf ears."*

Me: *"Touché. Uh, Jo-Jo, what are you eating?*

Jo-Jo [mumbling, as pieces of food spray from his mouth]: *"A salami sandwich. I didn't have time earlier."*

Me: *"Oh, were you too busy reading the latest fantasy news?"*

Jo-Jo: *"No, I was too busy making this salami sandwich. There's more to it than just salami."*

Me: *"Back to Dirk. Any words of wisdom?"*

Dirk: *"Losers think they're winners. Winners know they're winners."*

Me: *"You're a beautiful man."*

Jo-Jo: *"Me?"*

Me: *"Finish your sandwich."*

31

Dirk had to run moments later; one of his sports writer friends was getting ready to interview the surgeon who just operated on a prominent WR's knee. Dirk is getting an advance transcript of the interview before its publication later this evening, meaning he will know this player's likely recovery period and future value before any competitors do. That's *kick-ass*. That's Dirk.

And Jo-Jo? He was getting sleepy, so I put him in a cab and sent him home.

Being around Jo-Jo today reminded me of something Dirk said: "Losers think they're winners." Some of the worst fantasy managers think they are great managers. And that is the trap. When Jo-Jo gets a lucky win, he thinks it stems from his own brilliance. He is the guy who picks up and starts a decent DST without realizing that it is facing a very high-scoring offense on the road. One week this strategy works: In the first quarter, the high-scoring offense's QB is knocked out of the game. The backup QB has not faced a live defense since his senior year of high school six years ago. He proceeds to throw two picks and gets sacked four times. The next day, Jo-Jo brags to his friends that he just "*knew* my defense was gonna rock!" But he didn't. No one did. No one could have. So he continues to make flawed decisions, with a success rate just barely high enough to mask the inherent shortcomings in his approach to decision making.

Publicly Jo-Jo pretends not to care much about fantasy sports. But deep down he wants to prove to everyone how great he is. After a loss, he is a pathetic sack of shit. It is never his fault; the players sold him out. "My guys suck" is a common refrain. As a result, he might drop several of them—a couple of whom are terrific players who are off to inexplicably slow starts. Or he will complain about his players' tough schedules—something he could have researched before the draft. But why plan ahead when you can complain from behind?

Jo-Jo applies too much value to completely insignificant or wrongly identified situations. While watching his star WR catch only three balls for 45 yards while dropping two others passes, he is prone to say, "That guy is useless," without attempting to understand why the receiver fell short of expectations. Is the ball slick from rain? Is the QB facing more pressure than usual, thus throwing through a crowd or off his back foot or on the run, and therefore missing otherwise easy targets? Yes, these factors could foretell future challenges for the star WR. After all, if he is measurably less effective playing in the rain, or if the offensive line cannot protect its QB against even half-decent pass rushes, then Jo-Jo holds valuable information affecting future roster decisions. But he does not think this way. Instead he draws general conclusions about his players' worth and then searches for a replacement.

Over the years I have observed countless outliers in fantasy sports—events that are unexpected and unusual. I also have observed innumerable trend lines—events that frequently presage future results. Jo-Jo cannot tell the difference.

Dirk can.

So if you would rather be like Dirk, read on.

CHAPTER 5

FIELDING/FINDING A LEAGUE
YOU CAN DOMINATE

"I want you to be concerned about your next door neighbor.
Do you know your next door neighbor?"
– Mother Teresa

Fantasy victory begins, naturally, at the beginning. Some folks think that is Week 1; others believe it is draft day. In actuality, it is the moment you commit to a league—one of the most important decisions you will ever make, and one that requires absolute mastery.

Some rookies gleefully join five or more fantasy leagues simultaneously, devoting minimal time to each and hoping to get lucky in just one. Other neophytes join online "premier" leagues, paying sizable entry fees to compete against some of the brightest and most experienced fantasy minds in the business. Even seasoned Jo-Jos fail to spot the warning signs, leaping head first into the same competitive league where they have never made the playoffs, yet strangely believing that "this is the year." These people are morons, and I love it when they join my league.

So to field a league you can dominate, first find a bunch of morons, or at least people who, unlike you, don't care a helluva lot about fantasy sports. You should know many of them already. They are your slacker friends who get lit up every time they light up, which is hourly. They are your artist friends who are so deep and sensitive and creative that they would rather finish a series of all-blue paintings on all-white canvases than set their lineups on time. They are your shady friends who constantly seek shortcuts, almost always leading to fantasy failure. They are your celebrity friends tied up on the set of their latest lame movie or TV series, pretending to care about their silly little friends and your silly little league.

Other prime beat-down candidates include ER doctors, most of whom perform admirably in hospitals but dreadfully on game days. For that matter, any friends with at least semi-regular non-fantasy Sunday commitments are wonderful additions to any league. What better way to ensure they miss late-breaking injury news or useful in-game action and analysis?  U.S. presidents, senators, governors, and other elected officials make terrific opponents, as their minds usually are on spending your hard-earned donations on campaign key chains. And if you know any trial lawyers, get them on board; if you don't, try their 1-800 number plastered all over town. They are accustomed to taking a position and trying to prove its validity, rather than analyzing data objectively. As a result, they are apt to make irrational decisions throughout the season, such as defending the indefensibly futile QB they drafted way too early.

Although adding a few strangers to your league is acceptable, make sure a majority of members are friends, neighbors, or acquaintances—the fantasological novices you have encountered via work or church or your local Tuesday night bowling league. After all, playing with too many complete strangers poses certain risks, such as the possibility that they will collude against you through trades or rule changes, withhold your prize money, or kick you out right before the draft to make room one of their buddies. Associations, whether personal or professional, help ensure credibility and accountability. So stop placing newspaper ads that read, "Looking for people to play fantasy with me." With a few well-placed calls, you will find plenty of lovable losers knocking on your door.

If joining an existing league, verify that it is well organized, that the commissioner is at least somewhat experienced, and that the rules are very, very clear. Several years ago I was nearly denied six points when my DST's field goal coverage team returned an errant kick attempt for a TD. When my online league failed to register the points, I promptly told the commissioner that according to league rules, six DST points were awarded for all defensive and special team TDs. Since the commissioner could not refute logic, he overruled the pre-existing system and awarded me the points. These errors occur more frequently than you realize. No website is infallible. So find a league that anticipates such mistakes and has procedures in place for correcting them.

As stressed earlier, your league's parameters should be well suited for a *kick-ass* strategy of inserting undervalued players into your weekly lineup. If you are stupid enough to compete in a 20-owner, 16-player-per-team league (320 total players) comprising QBs, RBs, WRs, TEs, Ks (kickers), and DSTs, then good luck spotting high-impact free agents during the season (except through injuries and demotions). Under a scoring system using only these positions, there would be approximately 244 players each non-bye week (and obviously fewer when some NFL teams are on byes) with a realistic chance of helping your team. Competing in a 16-team, 12-player league (184 total players), for example, means that up to 60 potentially undervalued free agents would be available during non-bye weeks, and about 15 to 30 potentially undervalued free agents during bye weeks. Some of these players could be a weekly top 10 positional scorer. So joining a 16x12 league would give you the resources to achieve *kick-ass* fantasy success. If you find a comparably sized league that adds defensive players to the scoring mix, then even better, you would have more free agent pickups from which to choose.

Next, arrange casual encounters with each opponent so you can discover what makes them tick. What are their views on God? Were they abandoned by their parents at a young age? Are they ticklish? Once they are comfortable conversing with you, prod them for the really useful stuff like favorite and least favorite football team/players, underrated/overrated athletes, etc.

Imagine entering the draft knowing which owner is more likely to take or avoid which players in various rounds. With your selection five picks away, you might know with relative certainty whether your top targeted player remaining will fall into your lap, or whether you should trade up if he is likely to be snagged by the guy picking right before you. More specifically, suppose you are pursuing a QB who was suspended for a month last season for steroid use, and the guy whose back-to-back picks are sandwiched between yours is a Drug Enforcement Administration agent. Are you now more confident that your DEA buddy will bypass such "damaged goods," giving you the freedom to select a different highly targeted position player now, and then grab the QB on your next pick? Such insights give you a competitive edge over everyone else in the room.

Know each opponent's talent level. How have they fared in past seasons? Fierce competitors can finish at .500 even with crappy teams and rarely fall out of contention until late in seasons, while bad competitors might have a lucky season or two, but also will endure some pitiful years. The latter group includes people you can take advantage of through unfair trades and mind games throughout the season. Who thinks about this stuff? *Kick-ass* players do.

And whether you are searching for a league or starting your own, **do not be the commissioner.** As highlighted earlier, at least 50 hours per week are required for *kick-ass* fantasy managers. You have no business adding another responsibility to your plate—one that won't earn you respect or put money into your pocket. At best it is the most meaningless résumé builder after "conversational Latin" and "juggling." At worst, dumb competitors might blame you for everything from the scoring system to the playoff schedule to any swaps that appear to favor you. (As you will learn in Chapter 21, while *all* trades should be in your favor, being commissioner puts a target on your back.)

Likewise, you don't need the hassle of having to justify free agent pickups. One year I added a slightly injured and underperforming WR (a perennial top 25 talent) only a few minutes after a newbie manager gave up on him midseason. Despite complaints from a couple of jealous owners, their futile outcry paled in comparison to what commissioners I know have dealt with under similar circumstances—including sacrificing their own interests simply to quell an escalating league mutiny against what should have been heralded as a savvy free agent acquisition.

And that, dear readers, illustrates why your job is to be neither an administrator nor a compromiser. Your job is to win, and only to win.

PART II

THE PRESEASON

Famous Days in Fantasy Football History

September 13, 2010

One day after the Houston Texans' Arian Foster runs for 231 yards and three touchdowns in Week 1, derivatives trader and **Moore Wins Than You** owner Ralph Moore swaps the "one-hit wonder" for perennial top 10 fantasy scoring running back Ryan Grant of the Green Bay Packers. Sadly, Mr. Moore is vacationing in Prague without Internet access, so he is unaware that Mr. Grant got hurt in Week 1 and is out for the season.

Mr. Foster would finish the season as the league's #2 overall fantasy scorer. Mr. Moore would never vacation again.

CHAPTER 6

FLY SOLO OR PARTNER UP?

"There is no 'i' in team, but there is in win."
– Michael Jordan

Your old college buddy calls you one night. You pledged the same fraternity, roomed together all four years, got wasted every weekend, briefly dated the same conjoined twin, and twice accidentally set fire to your poor friend Rob (he's fine). He says, "Dude, I just joined a fantasy league. We gotta team up."

Not much of a dilemma, right? Of course you team up! It'll be great! Lately you two have been out of touch, and this will give you an excuse to talk all the time, just like in the old days. You have acquired a brother-in-arms, an extra brain, and another pair of eyes to watch games and track players. It is you and your friend against the world: the greatest fantasy minds bonding into a totally awesome superhuman organism, sharing in every success and dramatic turn. Perfect synergy. A perfect life.

But before accepting your buddy's collect call, recognize that a Devil's pact awaits. Until a few years ago, I teamed with no one. It always had worked for me, so why change? But then, at the constant urging of two great college friends, I joined their team for the first of three seasons— initially as a mere advisor, and then as a fully invested partner. Our union eventually dissolved after I realized they never would adopt my *kick-ass* philosophy.

One anecdote typifies the numerous challenges we faced. In the beginning, the three of us required unanimity for any roster or lineup change, believing this would ensure smart moves while simultaneously preventing in-fighting. However, this strategy did not function as designed. In August 2009, the Saints' RB situation was murky. Perennial RB fantasy stud Deuce McAllister had just retired, clearing the way for perpetually underperforming RB Reggie Bush to play a major offensive role. New Orleans had signed effective RB journeyman Mike Bell to compete for carries, and he was eyed by some fantasy team owners as a potential starter thanks to a stellar preseason. But my focus was on third-year pro Pierre Thomas. Battling a knee injury and heavy competition, he went undrafted in many leagues, including ours.

Not long after the draft, I called one of my partners and said, "We need to grab Pierre Thomas. He might not be useful now, but he could help us down the road." My friend advised me to call our other teammate to see what he thought. So I called partner #2, left a voicemail message, and waited. By the time he called back several hours later, one of our opponents had already picked up Thomas. Despite not making serious fantasy contributions until Week 3, this widely underappreciated and undervalued RB finished the season ranked 20th in fantasy points at his position—a solid #2 RB in our 12-team league. We missed out on his production not because of ignorance, but because our team was too unwieldy to make decisions quicker than the competition.

After this debacle, my partners and I agreed to base future moves on a simple majority: if two people thought Option A was best, then we went with Option A. As I soon realized, Option A could be the most inane decision imaginable. Yet if two people liked it, it was a done deal. And of course, I usually was the one pushing for Option B instead, meaning I continually had to bite the bullet and move on, even as our team's losses kept mounting. If you are the weak link on a three-person team with little to contribute substantively, then enjoy the ride. But by choosing to read this book, you value yourself too highly to put yourself in this situation. You want to be the strongest link—the guy who does his homework and makes the right moves at the right time. This approach makes sense if your two teammates always defer to you. But then why team in the first place?

Two-person teams are not much better. You want to pick up WR A while your pal insists on WR B. Who breaks the tie? I rest my case. Most two-person teams produce a leader and a follower—sometimes maintaining these roles throughout the season, and sometimes alternating as conditions warrant. After enduring teammates' misguided picks for too long, I now refuse to be a follower, ever. I also have no interest in adding a teammate who simply does what I want and then takes half the credit.

Guys like Jo-Jo Mc'scuses team up because they don't have time to manage their own roster:

Me: *"Jo-Jo, why are you so busy?"*

Jo-Jo: *"Time gets away from me, I guess. What with work and sleep and* Dancing With the Stars, *it's nice to know Willy is helping with research and making decisions."*

Me: *"Who?"*

Jo-Jo: *"Willy Waddle. He's nice to me at work, so I asked him to be on my team."*

Me: *"Has he made a lot of good decisions so far?"*

Jo-Jo: *"I guess so. We talk about once a week, and he tells me who we should pick up, and then I do it. We are 3-5 and not yet mathematically eliminated from the playoffs."*

Me: *"Do you make any decisions for the team?"*

Jo-Jo: *"Oh sure. If he forgets to call me, then on Sunday morning I log in and see if we should make any changes."*

How many penalty flags did you see, not including watching *DWTS*? Let's break it down:

(1) "Time gets away" from Jo-Jo. Becoming a fantasy winner requires using time to your advantage. When considering a partnership, ask

43

yourself whether this friend is punctual for appointments like job interviews or pedicures. Does he stay on top of his finances? Does he play video games until all hours of the night and then walk around in a stupor all day? You need someone who is focused, someone who knows how to budget his time to get the most out of his fantasy day.

(2) Jo-Jo does not know whether Willy has made good decisions. Partnering means owning up to mistakes. Gently but firmly reminding your friend that his last four roster moves sucked will help motivate him to do better next time, as well as strengthen your standing as the team's primary decision maker.

(3) When Willy is too busy to call, Jo-Jo waits until game day to set their lineup, foregoing numerous free agent pickup opportunities along the way.

I am not insisting that team play is an automatic recipe for disaster. If you know your respective roles, do your job, and fearlessly hold each other accountable, then you might become champions. In the first half of 2008—our first season together—my three-headed team seemed invincible. We collaborated on a draft strategy that yielded undervalued picks, culminating in an 8-0 record to start the season in our 12-team league. In case you are new to this, 8-0 is a rarity in fantasy football. Chances are, a few of your players will crap out during the same week, or a few of your opponent's players will enjoy dominant performances at the same time. Through eight weeks, armed with a top five QB, two top 10 RBs, three top-10 WRs, a top five TE, and the #1 DST, we had guided our squad halfway toward fantasy nirvana: perfection.

And I still reminisce about the three of us watching Monday Night Football in Week 9, mic'd up through our XBOXes from three separate cities. It was garbage time, as the game's outcome had been decided long ago, but not in our fantasy league, where we were tied when the trailing Redskins got the ball back with 2:28 to play. Maintaining our undefeated season hinged on our TE, Chris Cooley, picking up five more receiving yards. The 'Skins marched downfield. We cursed at our respective TVs as QB Jason Campbell hit Devin Thomas, Clinton Portis, and Antwaan Randle El. The clock continued ticking down. All seemed lost. And then, with under a minute left, Cooley caught a magical 13-yard pass, giving him 78 for the game and handing us a one-point victory.

Yes, there are special moments when you are grateful to be in it together. My friends and I were now an inconceivable 9-0. But if success easily brings people together, misfortune just as easily drives them apart. We went on to lose several games that season and fell just short of the title. In 2009 we missed the playoffs altogether. In 2010 we were even worse. Alas, my friends are not *kick-ass* managers. They prefer family, friends, and late-night Taco Bell runs to fantasy championships. Despite being good people, they are content to play fantasy football merely "for the fun of it." That is crazy talk, and by now hopefully you recognize that.

As a *kick-ass* player, I don't need male bonding or pats on the back or late night pillow fights. All I need are a set of rules, a confined universe of players, and some competitors with asses to kick. As the sole manager of my team, I do all the research, make all the decisions, and get all the credit when I win. Fantasy success cannot be maximized through compromise, as compromise is merely a time-share among good and bad decisions. I prefer maintaining a singular dedication to excellence, knowing that my decisions almost always will be better than those of any potential partner.

You might hear cockiness. In my ears, it is the sweet sound of a man who controls his own destiny. Ask yourself whom you would trust with your life: Your wife? Child? Spiritual advisor? Now ask whom you would trust with your *fantasy* life. Will your wife search for a worthy backup QB while you are stuck at the dentist? Will your child cut school to scan fantasy news reports all day? Will your spiritual advisor visit your local NFL team's practice facility to observe whether your injured #1 RB is participating in contact drills?

A *kick-ass* player is fully understood only by other *kick-ass* players. Our system of morality is based on a deliberate, unyielding pursuit of victory. Our language is a series of codes like TE 1, RB 2, and WR 3/4. When working in the same office with a league competitor, a *kick-ass* player never discusses sports openly, lest the opponent overhears and picks up vital information. When passing on the street, *kick-ass* players never make eye contact, but rather nod at each other's shoes to express their ephemeral humility. When invited to a *kick-ass* groom's wedding, they present him with a heaping bowl of cash, symbolizing the bounty he will receive in the upcoming fantasy season. There are 99 such rules of *kick-ass* conduct—one for each fantasy victory we all hope to achieve in our lifetime.

That is why we prefer to play alone. No one else understands our purpose, methods, or will to win. Greatness has its price, though the benefits are far more substantial, such as prize money. Flying solo means you keep all of it. I spend some of mine on my wife's birthday or anniversary present; she gets to choose which one we celebrate.

CHAPTER 7

BRACING OTHERS FOR WHAT'S TO COME

"I have frequently been questioned . . . how I could reconcile family life with a scientific career. Well, it has not been easy."
– Marie Curie

When my future wife and I started dating, I was a bit coy about my love of sports. But by day two, my self-restraint gave way: "Sorry I didn't tell you about my nearly year-round commitment to fantasy sports during our e-Harmony exchanges." My many ensuing fantasy victories certainly have made me a better husband. I'm sure in time she will agree.

When committing to becoming a *kick-ass* fantasy player, you owe it to family, friends, and associates to be upfront about your life's mission. They will find out eventually, such as when they find you on the living room couch on NFL Sunday for 11 hours, or under the covers with your laptop at midnight tracking NBA in-game stats, or live on ESPN discussing the upcoming MLB season with Chris Berman. Fantasy sports will not always be there for you. The occasional players' strike, owners' lockout, and, as we will discuss later, All-Star Game break create vast emotional chasms not easily filled. During these dark hours, you will need a shoulder to cry on, a compassionate friend who will listen, or a co-worker who will take your mind off it by giving you some meaningless assignment.

So before each fantasy season, always share with others how much they mean to you, and respectfully request their support and patience during the coming months. They must understand that this is not "good-bye," but rather "good-bye for a significant amount of time." They will appreciate your sincerity and thoughtfulness, and will think of you fondly when you are no longer available to make dinner, join them on vacations, attend staff meetings, or earn a steady paycheck.

Even if you have not been upfront with those who matter most, it is never too late to brace them for the life you are about to lead.

Significant Other

This section applies to any loved one with whom you are married or in a serious, monogamous relationship. Since I have a wife, I will use "wife" for all references to significant others. Feel free to mentally insert the name of your relationship partner, or skip this section if you are single and proud.

A week before your fantasy season begins, take your wife to a romantic dinner and break the news in public so she won't make too much of a fuss. Your spouse might say, "But you're already in a baseball league. Don't you want to focus on that instead of trying to juggle football, too?"

To which you will reply, "This is what I do." You must be firm here. Fantasy sports loyalty knows no wiggle room.

Then your wife invariably will ask you not to abandon your son, Jake, as he wrestles with first grade jitters, school bullies' daily taunts, and a recurrence of eczema. "He needs you more than ever."

To which you will reply, "What he needs is a father who finishes what he starts." Then regale her with tales of past fantasy glory, emphasizing life-affirming lessons learned along the way. Explain that your commitment as a loving partner will grow stronger after another brief return to your fantasy roots. And lastly, read to her from your love poem collection, in which you compare her to a 100-yard TD pass from your QB to your #1 RB, or some other *kick-ass* play that would be so amazing to see if you were actually watching a game right now instead of being stuck in a restaurant that is too fancy to carry TVs. Where's the waiter? I need the damn check. Tell her to go start the car. No wait, tell her to pay while you get the car, then pull in front and honk until she comes out. Where's the waiter??!!

Children

I hope to have children someday. When not distracting the shit out of people, they are tolerable. Regardless of age, they will understand and respect your passion for fantasy sports, because you will explain repeatedly that "Mommy and Daddy don't fight when Daddy is watching football." You will delight in their cheery disposition every time you grab the remote control. Two TV's in the house? Your precocious progeny will learn to record games upstairs so you can watch later. Errands to run? He will gleefully hop on his bike and won't return until the job is done, even if it takes all night.

Why bother cooking when there is so much fantasy work to do? With a recipe in hand and at least a second grade reading level, kids make great game-day chefs. After they have finished in the kitchen, invite them to watch with you. But don't let them crowd you on the couch; instead invite them to watch from *behind* the couch.

Remember, your #1 priority is fantasy success. Each time one of your children facilitates (or does not interfere with) such success, she/he shifts ever closer to the heralded #2 position. Once they embrace this concept, you have completed your child-rearing responsibilities while simultaneously preparing the little ones for a life of fantasy glory.

Other Family and Friends

If you are cursed with having a large, close-knit family—aunts, uncles, nieces, nephews, first-through-third cousins, and numerous siblings of unknown paternity—there is no time to appease them all. Likewise for friends who shun fantasy competition. Annual Thanksgiving touch football game with your old high school buddies? Not unless it starts around dawn or midnight EST, because there are three games that day that actually matter, and "amateur hour" on a muddy field is not one of them. On game days, the only sweating I will conceivably do is sweating out a victory over fierce competition. Sunday brunch to celebrate your mom's birthday? Make it Monday breakfast. On game days, I only celebrate yards, TDs, and defensive turnovers—and yes, 50+ yard field goals, because Ks matter more than most people realize (see Chapter 9).

To prepare family and friends for your impending absence, change your voicemail greeting to something like "I'm largely unavailable for the coming months. Please call again in January—or December if I can't find a decent quarterback off waivers." Similarly, create a few e-mail auto-responses such as "Sounds great," "Right back atcha," or "Happy Columbus Day!" You are not being selfish. On the contrary, they are being selfish for contacting you during fantasy season. You simply are maintaining a semblance of cordiality while pursuing your life's calling.

Co-workers

There are two kinds of jobs in this world: those that conflict with live football games and those that don't. If you are in the former camp, trudging into the office every Sunday afternoon to help your boss prepare reports for oh-so-important client meetings that week, then good for you. And if you compete in my league, I look forward to destroying you.

But there is also a more nuanced yet critically important distinction to the latter camp that separates the Hardys from the Mc'scuses. While you might work in a seemingly ideal Monday-through-Friday, nine-to-five job, how much time are you wasting on actual work, when instead you should focus on improving your fantasy team? Jo-Jo is terrified of questioning authority: his boss, parents, priest/rabbi/shaman, supposed online fantasy "experts," and so on. Self-doubt and fear  perpetually hold him captive. He wastes valuable office hours trying to look busy and maybe even does good work. But at what cost?

If you would rather be a *kick-ass* fantasy performer than a dime-a-dozen laborer, you owe it to your employer to set clear ground rules. Of course, that does not mean coming clean about your fantasy sports obsession. Instead explain to her/him that you are "going through a tough time in your life" (which is true, because fantasy failure is hard to accept) and you "need Ralph and Janet to cover your responsibilities while you recover." (Ralph and Janet are two of your toughest league competitors; you have just strengthened your hand while weakening theirs.) Then treat your co-workers to a tasty-yet-sensible snack break in the office lounge, and thank them in advance for giving Ralph and Janet the opportunity to shine in their new roles while you "invest all the time and energy needed to heal body and soul."

<u>Vendors</u>

Postal workers . . . dry cleaners . . . dog groomers. These are some of the many people you might have to deal with to keep your household functioning. After a fantasy loss, I don't want to talk to anyone. I don't even want to see anyone. My anguish defies words. God help those who cross my path.

Yet no matter how upset you are, do not piss off the people who keep the world rotating. A lost letter, a ruined suit, and a hideously shaved mongrel are potential by-products of fantasy-induced verbal tirades. It is not your fault, however. When your #1 WR breaks his leg in the first quarter while your opponent's defense scores more TDs than your QB, you deserve a venting session—but not at the expense of superior customer service.

So before Week 1, sit down with the vendors you plan to talk to over the next four months. Tell them you have a twin. This twin is a nasty little fucker. He frequently skips taking meds on Sundays, Mondays, Tuesdays, Thursdays, and Fridays. He should be handled very patiently and gingerly, so as not to cause a Huffington Post-reported incident.

You now have absolved yourself of any future wrongdoing, and are free to act like an asshole during and after bad weeks without any repercussions.

Other Acquaintances

Kick-ass fantasy players have no business keeping acquaintances who possess no material value. Bid farewell to that neighbor with whom you occasionally engage in small talk when returning from work. Continue to ignore that fraternity brother whose Facebook messages you have disregarded for years. And stop feeling obligated to chat with that sweaty, short dude you keep running into at parties. The smaller your social circle, the wider your fantasy path to victory.

*   *   *

Is this approach too stringent for you? Worried about alienating those who have supported you all these years? It is time for some tough love, people. If you want to win, there must be sacrifices, and I don't mean lambs—though if you have one handy and believe in an old-school Almighty, go for it. Fantasy sports competition requires full-blooded commitment, not half-blooded resignation or quarter-blooded procrastination. Allow it to penetrate your mind and overtake your senses. Paraphrasing Psalm 23, let it restoreth your soul, so that goodness and mercy shall follow you all the days of the season, and you shall dwell at the top of the standings forever.

After bracing others for what's to come, you will enter the season with a clear conscience and an empty heart, to be filled with acquired knowledge and a love of oneself. And that is the magic of fantasy sports.

CHAPTER 8

PICKING A TEAM NAME THAT DOESN'T SUCK

"All they had to do was put my name on a marquee
and watch the money roll in."
– Gloria Swanson

You have now joined a league, warned everyone to keep their distance, and cleared your schedule for the next several months. It is time to select a team name that doesn't suck.

In an attempt to be far too clever, you spend hours concocting the wittiest name you can think of. Moments after entering this name on your league website, you eagerly await the inevitable "Brilliant" and "I can't believe you're so brilliant" e-mails from your opponents. But they never come, do they? No, they never come. And why not? Because you are not funny.

Still, there is hope. If you avoid the missteps that have damaged millions of reputations, you might be well on your way to a winning team name . . . and as a result, quite possibly, a winning team.

For starters, take the serious and simple route. Nothing you come up with will make people think you are God's gift to laughter. A good name is one that keeps you under the radar rather than incurring ridicule from opponents who don't understand your unique brand of humor.

One guy I often compete against is named Mark (not you, Mark; the other Mark). He is a fierce competitor with Dirk-like qualities offsetting a friendly demeanor. He is the kind of guy I love to beat because he always comes prepared and plays to win. You would like him.

Year after year Mark's names are effective because they are (a) just arcane enough to be interesting while (b) never veering into the "ha-ha, aren't I funny" category. People with silly team names are pathetic, like that friend or co-worker who makes asinine comments to get attention; sometimes we laugh, but generally we pity him for trying so hard. The opponents we respect and want to trade with are those who let their team, not their name, do the talking. So save yourself the embarrassment of creating a moronic moniker. This also extends to your team logo, which many online fantasy sites offer. The time devoted to photo-shopping the commissioner's head onto a donkey's ass should be invested instead in football research and analysis. Don't try to pass off stupidity as creativity.

Second, if you had a good team name last year, keep it. Who says you should keep changing handles? Sturdiness breeds familiarity, earning others' trust and respect. With victories under your belt, these trust and respect levels will grow. A strong name, combined with fantasy success, is an agent of intimidation. Fear and intimidation lead opponents to take needless risks, as they come to believe that is the only way to beat you. I have witnessed many people eschew an almost guaranteed eight or nine points from a middling RB or WR in exchange for a feast-or-famine waiver pickup, simply because they don't believe their current lineup is adequate. How do they know what they need? They don't. But they are intimidated into thinking they do. Usually, their gamble goes unrewarded.

Dumb decisions are not a direct result of an opponent's team name. But a winning team's consistent designation, over time, evokes something more than the name itself. Call it effective branding. Call it self-confidence. Coca Cola does not replace its name every year. The Nike *Swoosh* has not morphed gradually into a football wearing a Groucho Marx moustache and glasses (bad team logo idea, by the way). Fantasy football produces a mental undercurrent that sweeps through league owners, psyching out the weakest foes, falsely emboldening the mediocre Mc'scuses, and perpetually invigorating the Hardys. A static nickname helps to fuel this powerful force.

Below is a brief list of lame-ass names and why you must avoid both them and their kindred. Some of these handles *really have been used in actual fantasy leagues.* I am serious. Thousands (millions?) of fantasy players define themselves each year not by wins and losses, but by the self-deluding premise that they are amusing. At times it makes me pessimistic about the fantasy world our children will inherit.

The Winners
You love telling people how great you are. But home alone in the dark, you sob yourself to sleep while clutching your tattered Teddy Ruxpin.

The Athletic Supporters
You are a genius at word play! A Shakespeare for the modern age! And a nimrod for borrowing a pun that is older than the Bible . . . and not nearly as funny. Now go read from your *Mad Magazine* collection.

The Tom Brady Bunch
Okay, I think I get this. Wait, don't tell me. Okay, there's *Tom Brady*—I get that. He's a football player. And then there's . . . hold on . . . gimme another moment . . . to figure out . . . this riddle . . .

Big Balls
Not only do you have big balls, but now you have let the world in on your secret. Too bad you have only two to share. And too bad you are so transparently over-compensating for your latent sexual inferiority complex.

Hammer Time

Your team name each year since '91. You enjoy calling your opponent every Sunday, proclaiming, "U can't touch this" and "I'm 2 legit 2 quit," and then quickly hanging up and sighing contentedly while grabbing another extra-large handful of Cheetos. And you wonder why nobody has your number stored on their cell phone.

The Icky Shuffle

A throwback to pathetic touchdown celebrations. You are the lone Bengals fan in your league, eager to remind the world of your team's "glory days." You practice the Shuffle at home before bed each night so that you can present it to your friends at the annual Christmas party. But sadly, your dance performance looks less like a cocky celebration and more like a frantic walk of shame.

The Ed "Too Tall" Joneses
(or any other sports hero you will never meet)

By naming your team after your favorite player, you are showing every punk in your league that you are playing to win. This alone should intimidate them into forfeiting each game. And if they don't, you can always go home and write yet another letter to Mr. Jones asking what women look like up close.

The Mighty Morphin Flower Arrangers

You have taken the name of a classically endearing children's television show and turned it on its ear. How brazenly naughty. How sinfully decadent. How pathetic that you own the DVD and Blu-Ray box sets.

The Dynamic Duo

You have decided to co-own a team with your best bud in the world. Two great friends, one super squad—joined at the hip, fantasy-style. It will soon become apparent that you are too amazing for this league. And it is already apparent that you are too cheap to pay for separate teams.

Norfolk-in-Chance

You have gleefully buried a dirty sound in a series of clean words. You are so excited about your *awesome* name that you go home to brag to your girlfriend. But she just moved out.

*　　　*　　　*

At best, adopting a shitty name invites league managers' guffaws and ridicule. At worst, it destroys your edge by diminishing your self-esteem while enhancing that of each opponent. Stop the cycle before it starts. Select an under-the-radar name and logo that will keep your energies focused on the only thing that matters: winning.

CHAPTER 9

PRELIMINARY RESEARCH

"The road to easy street goes through the sewer."
— John Madden

Now I will share with you my methodical, deadly accurate approach to pre-draft fantasy research, most of which can be applied throughout the season. This elaborate process consists of preliminary research (explained below) and draft prep (see Chapter 10). Tempted as you might be, do not skip ahead to the next chapter. Effective draft research is a progressive process. Without first absorbing the lessons found in this initial stage, you will fail to maximize your returns during the second stage.

And remember that being a good researcher does not make you a good *fantasy* researcher. Discard what you think you know and prepare to be rebuilt.

League Rules

It is shocking how many people ignore critical details when glossing over their fantasy league's "Rules" page. This stuff should be read and memorized long before draft day. For example:

- How many active and bench players does each team have?
- Which positions must be filled, and what is the minimum and maximum number of players required at each position?
  - Impacts draft prep breadth and season-long research.

- How many other teams are in your league?
- What is the time limit for making each draft pick?
  - Enough time to propose trades and make counter-offers?
- If doing an auction draft, are $0 bids permitted?
- If doing a standard snake draft (taking turns, alternating the order in odd and even rounds), how high is your first selection?
  - Essential for determining whether to trade up or down.
- Is this a keeper league?
- What are the drop/add rules?
- Is there a weekly drop/add deadline, and if so, when?
- When do lineups lock each week?
- When is the trade deadline?
- Does each team receive an injury roster spot?
  - Essential to fill on draft day.
- Which weeks do the playoffs start and end?
- How many teams make the playoffs?
- What is the playoff tiebreaker system?
- How is the prize money distributed?

And don't forget about the scoring system: Has anything changed since last year, or is anything different than in other leagues to which you are accustomed? A few years ago one of my leagues altered receiving points from one every 10 yards to one every nine yards. "Big deal" you say. And that is why you are reading this book instead of writing it.

Suppose your #1 WR last season had 1,360 receiving yards and eight TDs. Let's assume your league awarded one point for every 10 receiving yards and six points for every TD. Let's also assume, for the sake of simplicity, that he netted exactly 85 receiving yards in each of his 16 games. As you can see below, this production would equate to 176 fantasy points over the full season. Again, I am using a more simplified approach to illustrate this issue. In actuality he probably surpassed 100 yards a number of times and fell short of 70 yards several times. But his average haul was 85 yards, so that is how we will configure his points.

Now suppose this year your league *ever so slightly* modifies its rules, awarding a point for every nine yards instead of 10. And let's assume that, once again, your star WR amasses 85 yards each game with eight TDs over 16 full contests. Comparing each point distribution scenario to *actual* QB fantasy scorers during the 2009-2011 seasons, how would each WR stack up?

WR Fantasy Points Per 10 Receiving Yards: Effect of One-Point Rules Change

	WR @ 1 Point Per 10 Yards	WR @ 1 Point Per 9 Yards
Receiving Yards (Per Game)	85	85
TDs (Season)	8	8
Fantasy Points	176	192
2011 Ranking Among QBs	16th (Tie)	13th
2010 Ranking Among QBs	19th (Tie)	15th
2009 Ranking Among QBs	19th	14th

As you can see, awarding one point per nine receiving yards would have made WRs demonstrably more valuable compared to QBs. Jo-Jo never wonders how such a conceivably small rule change could impact his overall draft strategy or decisions throughout the season. "So what if my WRs get about one extra point per week? Onward!"

But Dirk understands. And hopefully now you do, too. The table above illustrates why such a seemingly minor modification must influence your fantasy tactics. A one-point-per-10-yards policy means this high-caliber WR's fantasy points would have corresponded with the 16th to 19th best QBs. However, if we assume one point for every *nine* yards, this same WR would have ascended an average of four ranking spots versus QBs. In other words, this one-yard rule change should grant your future WRs—and TEs, as well as RBs who accumulate receiving yards—a modest yet meaningful boost in value compared to other positional players (e.g. QBs, Ks, DSTs, and most RBs), converting an otherwise fifth round WR 2 into, quite possibly, a fourth rounder.

This is why you must begin analyzing how rules— particularly rule changes—will impact how each position is measured and valued against all other positions. And on a grander scale, you must understand how current rules should shape your overall roster management strategy.

<u>Internet and TV</u>

It is 4:30 p.m. on Wednesday. While most people are knee-deep in boring thoughts about their job, family, or the latest Ang Lee film, your brain remains focused on fantasy football. Because you are committed. That is why you win.

This commitment requires constant Internet access, from which nearly all of today's breaking fantasy news emanates. Long before your league's draft, institute a hard-nosed strategy for accessing all pertinent fantasy football information in real time. Hand-held devices like an iPhone or Android are perfect for those 4:30 p.m. weekday announcements, such as a star TE's suspension, a QB's demotion, or a team's #1 RB being forced to split carries with his team's #2 RB. After assessing the potential ramifications of each news nugget, you can choose either to ignore it or make a roster/lineup change, depending on what will most likely improve your short- and long-term fortunes.

In addition to securing a 24-hour Web device, you should do something about that *basic cable* of yours. Tired of being forced to watch two 3-11 teams battle it out because you are too cheap to invest in a comprehensive NFL viewing package? For God's sake, man, "be the change you want to see in the world." (I am quoting Mahatma Gandhi for extra effect . . . and because even he could not have sat still for three hours watching bad football.) And yes, while these 3-11 teams matter if their players comprise half your team, the point is that you must acquire access to *all* NFL contests on game days. As you will learn in Chapter 15, watching your players and scouted players compete is one of the most productive ways to analyze your present squad's strengths and weaknesses and to evaluate future roster adjustments.

News Sources

I will not disparage you for clicking on your league's website to access the latest news on your team roster and free agents. But if that is your one-stop-shop for fantasy news, then shame on you for aiming so low. *Kick-ass* players win because of the quality *and* variety of their news sources.

Thousands of sites claim to make extraordinarily accurate weekly fantasy predictions. Some of these sites are very good. Many others are full of crap. Dirk Hardy never confuses one type with the other, because he has researched nearly all of them.

So during this initial research phase, determine which sites publish the most useful and accurate information the fastest. Review last season's reporting to assess various sites' qualifications. Are their posts and predictions based on first-hand knowledge gleaned from interviews and practice field observations, or second-hand news from other websites? Some sites are useful compendiums of fantasy news, provided they disseminate this material promptly after it strikes, and as long as they pull from multiple sources. But don't let them become *primary* sources.

First-hand news should be your primary resource throughout the preseason, regular season, and playoffs. The more first-hand information you acquire, the more timely and accurate your decisions will be. For example, I recently read on a fantasy website that a team's head coach "confirmed" that his young RB's snap count "will increase this week." Very useful news, right? Except when I clicked on the news item's original source—a newspaper article whose author had spoken directly to the coach—its message was different: The head coach, in fact, "suggested" that the RB's snap count "would likely increase this week."

"Suggested"? "Likely"? The first-hand article painted a very different picture than the second-hand report. And soon I found that most other second-hand sources got it wrong, too, transforming a mere probability ("suggested . . . likely increase") into an indisputable fact ("confirmed . . . will increase"). Reliance on faulty news leads to faulty roster decisions, potentially undermining your team's performance more often than you realize.

Other criteria to evaluate as you peruse various websites: When a #1 receiver was injured last year for several weeks, how accurately did each site predict which player(s) would benefit from the injury? Do they post breaking news during games, or do they play Monday/Tuesday/Friday morning quarterback? If your waiver rules permit pickups and drops at any time (to be counted toward next week's contests), game-day posts could be a boon to your title hopes.

Suppose you are watching one of the early Sunday games when an opponent's stud RB hurts his leg. Immediately after being a good sport and saying a prayer for his family and fantasy owners everywhere, you must assess the injury. How? By reading websites that cover on-the-field and locker room reports with messages such as, "We have just learned that RB A has a torn ACL." As a result, you know whether to add the backup RB before any opponent does. And how did you do it? By researching, compiling, and bookmarking the most accurate, timely, and informative fantasy websites ahead of time.

In some ways, Twitter is eating into the fantasy news website business, and for good reason. I have a few go-to sites for each sport. But Twitter compiles news briefs on nearly any player at any time—and almost in real time. Before the season starts, before the draft, even before draft prep, research which reporters cover each NFL team. That means the expert overseeing ESPN's Buffalo Bills beat; the guy divulging everything about the Cowboys for the *Dallas Morning News*; the team at KNBR in San Francisco responsible for the weekly in-game play-by-play. Start following these people on Twitter, because often they will hear news before your league website and most other secondary sites pick it up. Receiving a roster-impacting report even 10 minutes before your opponents will give you a leg up on everything from trade negotiations to championship-enhancing free agent acquisitions.

Challenging Conventional Wisdom

As I write this sentence (and add this parenthetical notation), I am reading Michael Lewis's *Moneyball*. Most of you know the story: With less money to spend on prized prospects than most MLB clubs, Oakland Athletics general manager Billy Beane sought a competitive advantage for his relatively small-market team. Rather than judging talent solely on the usual methods (hitting, hitting for power, speed, fielding, and throwing), he started incorporating unconventional measurements such as a batter's on-base percentage and a pitcher's ability to induce groundball outs, as well as devaluing universally sacred qualities such as tall/muscular hitters who hit home runs (while striking out a ton) and pitchers with 98 MPH fastballs (whose awkward motions are recipes for elbow and shoulder injuries).

Similarly, *kick-ass* fantasy performers see things differently than most people. For example, in any league with conventional scoring, managers rarely analyze Ks for more than five minutes, usually toward the end of the draft. Take an informal poll before the start of your next draft: "Anyone who has researched kickers before now, raise your hand." It would be utterly shocking if any hands went up. And it would be equally shocking if the other guys did not think you were a tool for asking such a stupid question. So don't. But understand that current conventional wisdom states that *kickers don't really matter*. And now understand the truth: kickers *do* matter. The question we must answer is "How much?"

The reality is that in standard scoring leagues, top-end Ks meaningfully improve your weekly scoring potential. Even second- and third-tier Ks can contribute to your success. Review the following table, which shows how the #1 and #10 fantasy scoring K's would have ranked if their points had been earned at a different position:

K Rankings Among Other Positions

	#1 Ranked K Points / #10 Ranked K Points	Rank Among QBs	Rank Among RBs	Rank Among WRs	Rank Among TEs	Rank Among DSTs
2011	176 / 128	#18 / #24	#8 / #24	#11 / #26	#3 / #5	#3 / #16
2010	141 / 111	#21 / #28	#16 / #25	#20 / #32	#3 / #5	#16 / #23
2009	147 / 118	#20 / #23	#14 / #26	#20 / #28	#5 / #9	#20 / #20
2008	143 / 123	#22 / #23	#19 / #23	#20 / #28	#2 / #2	#13 / #18
2007	140 / 116	#17 / #18	#14 / #21	#21 / #33	#5 / #7	#15 / #22
Average Rank Per Position		**#20 / #23**	**#14 / #24**	**#18 / #29**	**#4 / #6**	**#13 / #20**

In my 13-team fantasy league, we play two opponents each week to make things a little more interesting. That means there are 13 games per week in our 12-week regular season. Out of these 156 contests in 2011, seven were decided by two or fewer points. Another nine games were decided by three or four points. That's 16 outcomes—a shade more than 10% of our head-to-head matchups—decided by four or fewer points. In those contests, would you have preferred starting the season's highest scoring K or the season's 10th highest scoring K? The answer is obvious. The #1 K averaged three more points per game than the #10 K. For years to come, each of your fantasy seasons will feature several close head-to-head scores. Why needlessly handicap yourself by two or three points per game?

And to those who still insist Ks are "not worth my time," examine the rankings in the table above. If a little extra research means the difference between drafting the 14th best RB versus the 24th best RB, would you invest the time? What about the 18th best WR versus the 29th? Or the 13th best DST versus the 20th? The answer: of course you would. Because you are not Jo-Jo. You don't skate by on what you learned while wearing fantasy diapers. You have enough self-respect and commitment to excellence to draw conclusions based on facts rather than make assumptions based on unsubstantiated theories.

The prevailing *assumption* is that Ks don't really matter. The *kick-ass fact* is that, even when removing 2011 from the equation, top-flight Ks place significantly higher than 10th ranked Ks when compared to RBs, WRs, and DSTs, while the top 10 Ks align somewhat comparably to the top 10 TEs. So if you think drafting a #2 RB or #2 WR is important, then why overlook the NFL's most talented Ks, who average about the same fantasy points per game as these more universally beloved middle-tier position players? Why do most managers draft second- and third-tier TE's before the first K comes off the board? Why shun that which will make your team stronger?

Fantasy football's conventional wisdom is outmoded in countless areas. I have offered one example, with empirical evidence to substantiate it. But don't stop challenging baseless assumptions. Take the extra step and build your knowledge base.

Embracing Conventional Wisdom

"Huh? You just said conventional wisdom is bad. Why are you torturing my brain?" That is what you are thinking—that, and whether you should return this book to Amazon in exchange for the five-star nose hair trimmer. Fight the temptation. Your dangling whiskers will thank you.

I openly embrace conventional wisdom when it is verifiable through empirical evidence. Trust nothing until you have evaluated its legitimacy. Trust no one unless they show you first-hand results. Once again, let's use Ks for our example.

For an online blog called the Harvard College Sports Analysis Collective, Jonathan Adler reported the following in November 2009:

> *Conventional wisdom argues that field goal kickers will experience greater success indoors compared to outdoors—that domes are better for attempting field goals. The purpose of this brief analysis is to examine whether there is, in fact, an association between being indoors and kicking success.*

In conducting this study, Mr. Adler recorded all of the nearly 10,000 NFL field goal attempts between 1998 and 2008, separating them into five distance categories. Within

20 yards, indoor field goal attempts demonstrated no statistical advantage over outdoor attempts. However, "from distances of greater than 20 yards, being indoors is strongly associated with higher FG success. And the significance of this association appears to increase along with the length of the FG attempt." That is, until 50+ yard kicks, which indicated only a weak association between kicking indoors and field goal success.

Mr. Adler has provided a very important public service by statistically reinforcing the integrity of a widely held theory. It is now bankable information, as opposed to merely conventional wisdom. For kicks between 20 and 49 yards, indoor attempts are more likely to be successful than outdoor attempts by a statistically significant margin. For kicks over 50 yards, the margin is much smaller, but still quantifiable.

Your Jo-Jo competitors don't know which widely held theories are true and which ones have been debunked. Frankly, they don't care, as their lackadaisical approach to fantasy sports makes me want to vomit in every room of my house. Do not trust anything you learned as a Jo-Jo. During this pre-draft phase, seek a competitive edge . . . and then another . . . and then another, fostering a new world fantasy order that will keep you many steps ahead of competitors throughout this season and beyond.

Dirk never rests. If you want to win every year in any sport, neither should you.

The Huddle

Each of the next few chapters ends with *The Huddle*— a collection of statistical findings that will bolster your fantasy expertise. Read them with an eye toward how the results will improve your title hopes.

Does a team's scoring prowess correlate with more fantasy points for Ks? Among the five NFL teams with the fewest points scored in 2011, their Ks finished #21, #25, #28, #29, and #31 in fantasy scoring among their peers. Each of these Ks played in all 16 games, so they had every opportunity to contribute. Among the top four scoring NFL teams, their Ks finished #2, #5, #6, and #7 in fantasy points. (Note that two teams tied for the fifth most points scored; the Panthers' K finished #26 in fantasy points, while the Chargers' K finished #14 in fantasy points.)

Among the five teams with the fewest points scored in 2010, their Ks finished #8, #19, #23, #26, and #28 in K fantasy points. Among the top five scoring teams, their Ks finished #2, #3, #5, #6, and #14. (Note that the #6 scoring "K" actually was the combination of two Ks used by the same team [the Patriots], due to an injury midway through the season.)

And among the five teams with the fewest points scored in 2009, their Ks finished #12, #14, #18, #20, and #29 in K fantasy points. Among the top five scoring teams, their Ks finished #1, #2, #3, #7, and #11. (Note that the #11 ranking was the merging of two Saints Ks, while the #18 ranking was the merging of three Buccaneers Ks.)

Conclusion: Injuries, demotions, suspensions, and holdouts aside, there is calculable evidence that Ks playing for the highest scoring teams, on average, rack up a lot more fantasy points than Ks playing for the lowest scoring teams. Until or unless this trend changes, the pattern is consistent enough—and the gap wide enough—to incorporate these findings into your draft strategy.

CHAPTER 10

DRAFT PREP

"Use only that which works, and take it from any place you can find it."
— Bruce Lee

Now that you have studied the various implications of your league's rules, secured technological support, identified which Web resources produce the most useful information, and initiated your own study of the veracity of conventional fantasy football wisdom, you are ready to conduct research for your upcoming draft. During this next phase, you must focus all five senses on developing a vastly superior draft strategy. Take it from Dirk Hardy:

> *"With my left eye I read news stories, while my right eye stares penetratingly at player performance metrics. With my left ear I listen to team radio coverage in each NFC city, while my right ear listens to team radio coverage in each AFC city.*

"With my nose I smell someone who has not showered for days in order to maximize time spent researching and assessing fantasy players. With my tongue I taste Fritos crumbs and stains, licking my hands clean to keep them from damaging my laptop.

"And with my fingertips I dance along my computer keyboard and deftly maneuver the mouse, accessing any and all information while composing my master plan."

Dirk is not a jolly guy. But his intensity and drive serve a purpose. As with anyone envisioning a lofty goal, Dirk is methodical and unyielding in his pursuit. If forced to attend church, he brings reading material. When going to the bathroom, he brings a laptop. While dining with family, he keeps a pad of paper and pen next to his plate to jot notes. His powers of concentration have strengthened steadily in recent weeks, leading to this critical period necessitating hundreds of hours of labor to execute a nearly perfect draft.

Where do we begin? With a player matrix. Successful draft preparation requires compiling a comprehensive list of all positional players, which also will serve as your primary resource throughout the season. I recommend using an Excel document or something comparable for easy viewing and sorting. Include not only obviously draftable individuals, but also backup QBs, third-string RBs, #5 WRs, and #2 TEs. Your initial list should comprise almost 400 players. Assuming a larger-than-usual league of 16 teams with 15 players per team, such a collection will ensure more than 150 extra players.

Why so many? Among those 150+ castoffs, a few dozen will be useful spot starters throughout the season, about 10-20 will mature into quantifiable fantasy commodities by the latter half of the season, and a small handful likely will become the equivalent of fantasy gold: entities defying even the best prognosticators' wildest guesses. Consider the unheralded backup QB thrust into the spotlight after the All-Pro starter goes down for the season; the rookie WR expected to play solely on special teams, but whose acrobatic catches in Week 3 force the head coach to reconsider; or the vastly overachieving young DST that was supposed to be one or two years away from draftability. These and many other surprising scenarios play out every year. This is why you cannot afford to ignore any of them.

Next, record in your player matrix the depth chart for each team at each fantasy position. Even Jo-Jo Mc'scuses knows that some of these depth rankings—particularly among RBs and WRs—will change throughout the season. But you need a starting point. Create a column in your Excel document and number each player 1 through 5 (or through 6 or 7 if some teams' receiving corps are not fleshed out yet). Then mark all position battles. For example, a rookie RB and veteran RB might be vying for backup duties on a run-heavy team; grabbing the #2 spot could translate to 10-12 carries per game at some point during the season—and perhaps an occasional start depending on the #1 RB's weekly status. This is prime information to track, as the eventual winner might not be on opponents' pre-draft lists, but certainly could contribute on the fantasy scoreboard during the season. Tagging each position battle (as verified by news sources) will empower you to take calculated risks for under-the-radar, moderate-to-significant-upside athletes.

Identify which players are injured and the severity of each ailment (how many games they could miss, and whether the injury could negatively impact future performance). Each NFL player has at least one backup. As you will learn in Chapter 18, injuries equal opportunities. A #2 WR contending with turf toe or knee soreness in the preseason eventually could relinquish his starting job to the #3 WR, which instantly would place the latter player on many teams' waiver radars. Before the ailment turns into a changing-of-the-guard, remain ahead of the curve: track these developments and analyze their implications.

There is much healthy debate on whether contract issues affect player performance. Some fantasy owners maintain a little distance from players who have just signed lucrative long-term contracts, for fear that these fantasy contributors will be less motivated as a result. In a similar vein, some owners believe guys competing in the final year of their contract have more incentive to play well.

In reality, it depends on the player. Some athletes are "Dirks of the Turf," possessing an innate drive to succeed regardless of their personal/contractual situation. Their incentive to thrive is based less on money and more on a desire to play from their hearts, for their teammates and fans, and to win. Some fantasy managers perceive that other types of athletes—like those who hold out until their existing contract is restructured—care more about success off the field than on it. While I don't yet have empirical evidence proving that one type of player is better than another in the first/last year of a contract, I do base my selections on each player's historical data. Namely, if an athlete played better than usual in the final year of his first contract, I am more inclined to move him up a notch on my draft board when he enters the final year of his second contract.

But regardless of one's contract situation, I usually value Dirks of the Turf who underperformed the previous season, provided that their poor numbers were not due to (a) advancing age, (b) a chronic injury, or (c) an irreversible drop on the depth chart. While greatness cannot always be quantified, generally it can be identified. I am always searching for guys with chips on their shoulders and something to prove, as long as they possess sufficient talent that has been exhibited frequently during their careers. Maybe it is a WR who suffered a season-ending injury in Week 9 last year, finishing under 1,000 receiving yards and below seven TDs for the first time. If he is healthy, hungry, and still in his athletic prime, then I like his odds for returning to glory the following season

Or perhaps it is a 28-year-old QB who passed for a career-low 3,100 yards and 20 TDs last year, largely due to an unusually high number of receiver drops and a depleted OL (offensive line). But if his team signed a new #1 WR in the offseason, and if his starting OL is returning and is 100% healthy heading into the draft, then I likely will target this QB as an undervalued performer. Not everyone will thrive in these scenarios; if they did, fantasy football would be easier even for Jo-Jo. But by identifying these recently underperforming Dirks of the Turf, early round talent might fall into your lap as late as your draft's middle rounds.

OLs do not garner enough attention in many drafts. But after analyzing run and pass performances based on various OL preseason rankings, I have found that such data helps shape (albeit not always dramatically) fantasy projections. Am I saying a terrible RB will thrive behind a #1 OL? No, just as I am not promising that an All-Pro QB will be emasculated behind an injury-depleted OL. There are no guarantees in fantasy sports—only probabilities. And there is some probability that a team's OL preseason ranking will correlate with its offensive players' fantasy production, depending on these rankings' accuracy. Their level of reliability hinges on their source, as well as their degree of specificity.

If you are fortunate enough to find a trustworthy website that separates *run block* rankings from *pass block* rankings, congratulations. It is not easy, at least as of this book's publication. Over the years I have identified two such breakdowns on moderately dependable fantasy sports websites:

OL Rankings: Run Block / Pass Block

Prognosticator / Rankings Criteria	Top 10 Projected OLs – Run Block	Bottom 10 Projected OLs – Run Block	Top 10 Projected OLs – Pass Block	Bottom 10 Projected OLs – Pass Block
2009 ESPN / Scouts.com				
Avg Rush Yard Rank	12th	21st		
Avg Rush TD Rank	12th	23rd		
Avg Pass Yard Rank			16th	22nd
Avg Pass TD Rank			14th	20th
2007 FootballGuys.com				
Avg Rush Yard Rank	14th	19th		
Avg Rush TD Rank	16th	17th		
Avg Pass Yard Rank			18th	18th
Avg Pass TD Rank			14th	18th
Total *Combined Avg Rank*	14th	20th	16th	19th

Among the top 10 projected *run block* OLs, their teams finished their respective seasons with an average rushing rank (based on rushing yards and rushing TDs) of 14th out of 32 teams. The teams with the worst 10 projected *run block* OL's averaged a #20 ranking based on performance. By a narrower but still significant margin, *pass block* OL preseason rankings also were an accurate predictor of future passing/receiving success (based on passing/receiving yards and passing/receiving TDs).

So to FootballGuys.com and ESPN/Scouts.com, thank you. In seven of the eight examples shown above, their projected top 10 OL performers contributed to more average rushing yards and passing yards per game than their projected bottom 10 OL performers. And the one exception—average passing yard rank in 2007 compared to FootballGuys.com's OL *pass blocking* projections—ended in a tie. If you locate any reputable preseason OL rankings based on *run blocking* and *pass blocking,* incorporate these findings into your decision making.

A note of caution: If RB A and RB B appear equal, but RB A plays behind a fifth ranked *run block* line, while RB B plays behind a 28th ranked *run block* line, that is very useful information. But it does not mean RB A will produce more fantasy points this season than RB B. Examine how each rusher has fared in the past. If RB A performed ably while running behind a worse OL last season, and/or if RB B is accustomed to playing behind a better OL, then RB A appears to own a distinct advantage. However, if RB A has been a 1,000-yard rusher for three straight seasons while running behind a top-5 *run block* OL, then his exceptional OL this season does not give him a boost; it merely mirrors what he—and fantasy owners—have come to expect. Therefore, our study of rankings must incorporate the previous one or two years' rankings so that we can truly understand each affected player's potential.

If you are not lucky enough to find *run block* or *pass block* breakdowns, a simple OL ranking is better than nothing. Here are the preseason predictions I have tracked over the past few years, distinguishing between more accurate and less accurate OL projections. These general OL rankings do not provide the same clear-cut guidance as the previously identified *run block* OL rankings, yet are roughly as helpful as the aforementioned *pass block* OL rankings:

OL Rankings

Prognosticator / Rankings Criteria	Top 10 Projected OL's	Bottom 10 Projected OL's
2011 QuickFixSports.com		
Avg Rush Yard Rank	23rd	12th
Avg Rush TD Rank	20th	18th
Avg Pass Yard Rank	13th	22nd
Avg Pass TD Rank	13th	19th
2011 About.com		
Avg Rush Yard Rank	16th	19th
Avg Rush TD Rank	15th	20th
Avg Pass Yard Rank	17th	18th
Avg Pass TD Rank	13th	21st
2010 FantasyKnuckleheads.com		
Avg Rush Yard Rank	18th	14th
Avg Rush TD Rank	18th	14th
Avg Pass Yard Rank	17th	13th
Avg Pass TD Rank	15th	16th
2010 Yahoo! Sports / Fantasy Guru		
Avg Rush Yard Rank	14th	17th
Avg Rush TD Rank	15th	16th
Avg Pass Yard Rank	16th	22nd
Avg Pass TD Rank	13th	20th
2008 ESPN / Scouts.com		
Avg Rush Yard Rank	18th	16th
Avg Rush TD Rank	16th	19th
Avg Pass Yard Rank	12th	22nd
Avg Pass TD Rank	9th	19th
2007 ESPN / Scouts.com		
Avg Rush Yard Rank	15th	20th
Avg Rush TD Rank	11th	17th
Avg Pass Yard Rank	12th	18th
Avg Pass TD Rank	12th	20th
Combined Average Ranking	*15th*	*18th*

As you can see, not all rankings are equally useful. Who are FantasyKnuckleheads and QuickFixSports? Locate and analyze as many websites as possible, so that you can uncover which ones possess the most value. I gave Fantasy Knuckleheads a look in 2010, logging their OL projections and returning at season's end to record what happened. As it turned out, the other sites' preseason OL rankings more accurately predicted rushing and passing/receiving production. The next season I came up empty when searching for the Knuckleheads' 2011 OL rankings. Maybe they decided to limit their content to areas where they possess the most expertise.

Any resource might help lead you to victory. But not *every* resource. The more you explore, the more you will find. And the more you analyze, the more capable you will become at discarding unusable information and zeroing in on tools that will help you most. ESPN/Scouts.com's OL rankings strongly correlated with offensive stats in multiple seasons. But since they have not produced rankings in recent years, I have had to continue broadening my search. QuickFixSports.com might be worth some future looks. If its next predictions more closely reflect actual performance, its value will rise. If not, its value will fall. Identify, analyze, revisit, and (if beneficial) utilize. This is the process by which we uncover actionable material for the draft and throughout the season.

Some people pay too much attention to teams' "strength of schedule," while others pay too little. Its true level of importance lies somewhere in between. I have witnessed top-tier RBs post monster numbers against top-tier DSTs, just as elite QBs occasionally struggle statistically against weak DSTs. So how do we make sense of it all? By ignoring Jo-Jo's shortcut sensibilities and adhering to Dirk's admirable discipline:

Step 1: Research which offenses are expected to be the most explosive (based on your league's scoring system), and which ones likely will be the most inept. Separate into two groups comprising five to six teams each.

Step 2: Research which DSTs are expected to be the most productive (based on your league's scoring system), and which ones likely will be the worst. Separate into two groups comprising five to six teams each.

Step 3: Research which DSTs are expected to be the most productive *against the run* (based on your league's scoring system), and which ones likely will be the worst. Separate into two groups comprising five to six teams. Repeat these steps for predicted DST performance *against the pass*.

Step 4: Examine each team's schedule and record how many "difficult" (playing against the best offenses) and "easy" (playing against the worst offenses) matchups await each DST. Also note whether any of these potentially difficult or easy opponents will occur during your league's playoffs. Repeat for each position (QB, RB, etc.), calculating how many "difficult" games (versus the best run and/or pass defenses) and "easy" games (versus the worst run and/or pass defenses) await each player.

You'd better not be thinking what I think you are thinking: "But that means looking up schedules for all 400 players in my matrix! That will take forever!!" Boo-hoo. Would you like to call your mommy and tell her all about this mean ol' book? Or would you rather become a fantasy champion? Excellence requires time and patience. During my many years of fantasy success, complaining has been the furthest thing from my mind. So it should be for you, too. Prepare to win. Play to win. Then win. It is a simple concept embraced only by the toughest and most capable among us.

Now let's revisit schedule difficulty. Here is how to apply it during the draft and throughout the season. Applying all non-schedule criteria, let's say QB A and QB B are projected to finish with the same fantasy point total. Remember, you are basing this on superior research, not simply on a website you stumbled upon while hunting for an illegal download of *Remember the Titans*. Assume that QB A will face three of the projected top-tier defenses, while QB B will not face such difficult opponents. And assume that QB A will face only one of the projected bottom-tier defenses, while QB B will face three such easy opponents. So far, this aspect of the schedule favors QB B, in that he will match up against fewer great defenses and more bad defenses than QB A. Now let's fine-tune this analysis.

Suppose QB A will battle three of the projected top-tier defenses *against the pass*, while QB B will face no such pass-focused defenses. And suppose QB A will compete against one of the projected bottom-tier defenses *against the pass*, while QB B will match up against three weak pass defenses. This information is even more valuable because it strengthens your findings by narrowing your analysis. A great pass defense generally hurts QBs more than a great run defense, particularly pocket QBs whose yardage and TDs primarily come through the air.

Now suppose QB A will face the toughest *against-the-pass* defense during your league's finals, while in that same week QB B will face the third worst DST *against the pass*. This does not mean that QB A is worthless and QB B should be your biggest target. It only means that (a) you understand the matchups awaiting each player, (b) you will weigh these findings with other identified strengths and weaknesses, and (c) it is a long season, so it is impossible to predict in the preseason how a player will perform in weeks 16 or 17. While no single approach guarantees flawless results, by implementing dozens of effective approaches collectively, you will make wiser decisions.

Remember that while preparing for the draft, you have the capacity to learn nearly anything you want to, using historical statistics to test the likelihood of future behavior. Through such study, you can become a better fantasy competitor with a higher likelihood of winning your league. In a sense, you are a scientist seeking a cure for Jo-Joism. Let's say you are debating whether to rank RB A or RB B as the #1 RB on your draft board. Both are entering their fourth NFL season, are expected to handle the bulk of their respective team's carries, and are projected to amass around 1,400 rushing yards and 12 TDs. One distinction you have found is that RB A's team is projected to have one of the worst defenses in the league, while RB B's team made several defensive improvements in the offseason and now is considered a top five fantasy defense. Jo-Jo does not care how defensive numbers might correlate with offensive performance. But we know better.

It is time to put on your scientist hat, or smock, or whatever:

(1) Formulate a hypothesis. (e.g. "Teams that give up the *fewest* points in a season run the ball more than teams that give up the *most* points in a season.")

(2) Conduct research. (I have already done this, so kick back and relax.)

(3) Is there conclusive evidence? (Again, I have got this covered. Just follow my lead.)

Here is what I have learned: In each NFL season between 2001 and 2011, the five teams with the fewest PA (points against) averaged more rushing attempts than the five teams that surrendered the most points:

Season Rushing Attempts:
Top 5 PA Teams / Bottom 5 PA Teams

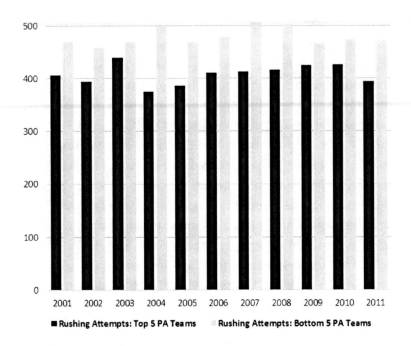

■ Rushing Attempts: Top 5 PA Teams   Rushing Attempts: Bottom 5 PA Teams

To be clear, I am not referring to *fantasy* points. These numbers are based on *NFL* points. It does not matter what league rules you use. NFL points are an American standard, like apple pie and Donkey Kong.

So I took this research a step further, discovering that in each season over this same 11-year period, the five teams with the most PA averaged more passing attempts than the five teams with the fewest PA:

Season Passing Attempts:
Top 5 PA Teams / Bottom 5 PA Teams

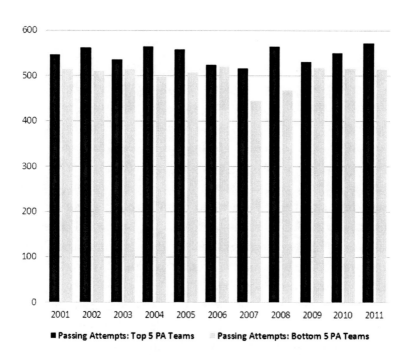

■ Passing Attempts: Top 5 PA Teams   Passing Attempts: Bottom 5 PA Teams

Let's break this down into easily consumable chunks: Between 2001 and 2011, the five highest PA teams (i.e. relatively bad defenses) averaged 25.5 rushes per game, while the five lowest PA teams (i.e. relatively good defenses) averaged 29.9 rushes per game. In no season did the five "bad" defenses collectively average more rushing attempts than the five "good" defenses. Therefore, there is a strong probability that RB A will enjoy fewer rushing opportunities in future seasons (approximately four fewer per game, if trends continue) than RB B. Therefore, all other things being equal, RB B will have more opportunities potentially to gain yards and score TDs.

A similar disparity exists in the passing game, affecting QB, WR, and TE (and to varying degrees, RB) performance potential. Between 2001 and 2011, the five highest PA teams (bad defenses) averaged 34.2 passes per game, while the five lowest PA teams (good defenses) averaged only 31.4 passes per game. That equates to nearly three extra passes per game for bad defensive teams.

Obviously this does not mean that only QBs on bad defensive squads and only RBs on good defensive teams are worth drafting; while they tend to earn more passes/rushes per game, further analysis is needed to determine whether they convert these bonus opportunities into positive fantasy points. But the fact is that these rushing and passing trends have not significantly wavered in 11 years, meaning the *opportunities* afforded to bad-defense-QBs and good-defense-RBs are consistently greater than for their counterparts. This is now bankable information, in that we can add it to our tool box as we weigh draft options.

Now shift focus to your league's fantasy scoring history. I cringe (and then privately celebrate) when someone drafts players based on some random "expert's" rankings, when such predictions often don't even correspond to your league's point system. I am referring to the John Does on famous sports websites who publish their "Top 100 Fantasy Players" list or "Top 20 Sleepers" rundown. Their stuff might be useful if you devote only 30 minutes to draft preparation. But if you want to start acting like Dirk, don't let these lists steer you off course. To be clear, **you cannot effectively rank fantasy players without weighing positional scoring rankings**. What do I mean? I will show you . . . right now.

Before ranking players, you have completed the first dimension of draft prep: assembling a player list. You also have wrapped up the second dimension: cataloguing depth charts, position battles, and psychological insights into various athletes. The third dimension consists of analyzing scoring tendencies for each fantasy position based on *your league's scoring*. I stress "your league" because you are merely comparing apples to snow globes when quantifying future performance based on anything other than the scoring mechanism you will use all season. For example, if your league awards one point per reception and the Web ranking you are gleefully eyeing does not, then these supposedly useful rankings are skewed. If you incorporate them into your draft strategy, you will want to pull out your remaining hair by Week 3.

Heading into my 2011 CBSSports draft, I examined past fantasy scoring tendencies for each of the six positions my league used, which were based on my league's scoring rules (six points per TD, one points per 10 rushing/receiving yards, etc.). The results, naturally, were illuminating:

2010 Fantasy Scoring Distribution per Position

	QB	RB	WR	TE	K	DST
Top 10 **Fantasy Scorers**	8	1	0	0	0	1
Top 11-30 **Fantasy Scorers**	6	6	5	0	0	3
Top 31-61* **Fantasy Scorers**	5	6	10	1	0	9
Top 62-100 **Fantasy Scorers**	5	7	12	3	5	7

* Disparate ranges due to ties in player point totals.

As you can see, QBs comprised eight of the top 10 fantasy scorers in 2010 (again, in *my league* using *my league's scoring*). One might conclude that upper-tier QBs helped level the playing field. After all, whether you selected the #1 or #8 QB, at least you snagged a top 10 performer. Or at least that is how Jo-Jo interprets these findings.

The other, more meaningful perspective is that the #1 QB scored 307 points while the #8 QB finished with 236. That 71-point chasm was the second largest gap (RBs produced the largest) between a position's #1 and #8 scorers. In 2009 that gap was 72 points. In 2008 it was 78. So yes, most elite scorers in 2010 were QBs. But by separating the elite talent from the next-in-line passers, a draft strategy emerges. Draft success requires you to seize elite talent and to recognize where each positional drop-off exists. For example, notice the top 10 overall scoring RB and DST in the table above. You certainly won't *know* which RB and DST will lead their respective position in fantasy points this year. But in these past two chapters, you have learned how to make more accurate predictions using historical data and detailed analysis. If 2010's positional scoring distribution is consistent year after year, then investing, say, your second round pick on your projected #1 DST likely would make your roster stronger than selecting merely the seventh or eighth best QB. Mind-blowing, huh?

The next tiers of rankings in the above table should be self-explanatory. Based on past positional performance you are more able to project future positional performance. Knowing where the elite WRs and TEs fall, understanding when it is time to snag the last upper-tier DST, sensing when a deadly accurate K on a high-scoring team should be plucked from the available player pool . . . these dilemmas are more easily solved when envisioning where they will rank among the top 100 fantasy scorers.

Now let's examine the 2009 and 2008 numbers:

2009 Fantasy Scoring Distribution per Position

	QB	RB	WR	TE	K	DST
Top 10 **Fantasy Scorers**	8	2	0	0	0	0
Top 11-30 **Fantasy Scorers**	7	4	7	0	0	2
Top 31-61* **Fantasy Scorers**	4	3	5	3	0	16
Top 62-101* **Fantasy Scorers**	3	14	13	3	6	1

Disparate ranges due to ties in player point totals.

2008 Fantasy Scoring Distribution per Position

	QB	RB	WR	TE	K	DST
Top 10 **Fantasy Scorers**	6	2	1	0	0	1
Top 11-30 **Fantasy Scorers**	5	7	3	0	0	5
Top 31-60 **Fantasy Scorers**	6	8	10	1	0	5
Top 61-101* **Fantasy Scorers**	5	6	13	0	11	6

Disparate ranges due to ties in player point totals.

From year to year there are clear differences in my CBSSports league's positional performances. But there are also remarkable similarities:

- QBs predominate in the top 10 scorers group.
- QBs, RBs, and WRs are more evenly distributed among the top 11-60 scorers.
- Some TEs rank as mid-upper-tier scorers (though their value grew in 2011, thanks to Rob Gronkowski, Jimmy Graham, and company).
- Several DSTs are among or nearly among elite overall scorers.
- Several Ks are among the top 100 or 101 overall scorers.

Imagine applying this historical scoring breakdown to your opponents' shock on draft day . . . and to their dismay as you coast to the league title. It has happened to me, and it can happen to you. The key is developing *kick-ass* instincts through effective first-hand research and analysis, and then trusting these instincts above so-called "expert" advice.

By now you should have at your disposal a broad array of online resources with which to research and analyze data. You have developed a player matrix, recorded depth charts, and highlighted injuries and team positional battles. You have factored in Dirks of the Turf, team schedules, OLs, running/passing potential, and other criteria. You have proposed hypotheses and dutifully sought to prove or disprove them. Your brain is filling with the most useful information it will ever need. Never stop filling it.

Before walking into the draft room, one step remains: developing a final rank-order of the roughly 400 players in your matrix, with projected fantasy points for each. These rankings should serve as guidelines, not as hard-and-fast judgments. As you will see shortly, flexibility is a key attribute of any successful drafter.

All notes accumulated throughout this preparation phase should be at your disposal, including which TEs are hurt, which WRs are no lock for starting jobs, which DSTs will compete against the most explosive offenses, and so on. This material must be easily accessible, distinguishable, and sortable. Note which player at each position is followed by a significant drop in projected fantasy points. For example, if you label QB's A, B, C, D, and E as top-tier performers, while QB F (the next ranked QB) is not expected to finish near that elite grouping, mark a division between QB's E and F. Repeat this process for each position for multiple tiers. During a draft, oncoming *talent chasms*—the shift from one tier of player to the next—remind us when to grab as many players from as many higher tiers as possible (more on this subject in the next chapter).

While I could write 500 pages on how to prepare adequately for a fantasy draft, my publisher won't let me. So start with my ideas and build on them. Do your own research. Discover your own strategic advantage. And kick ass.

The Huddle

I tracked all preseason fantasy rankings from ESPN (2009 and 2010 seasons) and CBSSports (2010 and 2011 seasons) to quantify their accuracy. As a *kick-ass* fantasy competitor, I wished to understand the extent to which their preseason rankings mirrored players' actual fantasy point totals that season. Both sites were, and still are, valuable resources in my continual pursuit of fantasy titles. However, we must always test resources to verify their usefulness; since no one can predict the future, no single fantasy tool is infallible—though some are better than others.

On the eve of Week 1 of each season, I logged onto these fantasy league sites and recorded their top 10 projected fantasy point scorers for the upcoming season at each of six positions: QB, RB, WR, TE, K, and DST. Based on their top 10 rankings (for 60 players overall), how well did each site predict *actual* end-of-season fantasy point rankings within each position? I could justifiably compare ranking projections to actual fantasy outcomes because the scoring system each website used for its predictions (i.e. six points per TD, one point per 10 yards rushing/receiving, etc.) was identical to the scoring system I used to quantify each player's total end-of-season fantasy points.

Therefore, among all players ranked in the preseason top 10 for projected fantasy scoring, what was their average fantasy scoring ranking (within their respective position) for the season?

Preseason Top 10 Predictions:
Average Positional Fantasy Scoring Ranking (Season)

	Average Positional Fantasy Scoring Ranking
2009 ESPN	12th
2010 ESPN	16th
2010 CBSSports	14th
2011 CBS Sports	15th

I also wished to discern how accurately each site predicted end-of-season fantasy point rankings based on their preseason projections for the top *three* players per position (18 players overall). So among all players ranked in the preseason top 3 for projected fantasy scoring, what was their average fantasy scoring ranking (within their respective position) for the season?

Preseason Top 3 Predictions:
Average Positional Fantasy Scoring Ranking (Season)

	Average Positional Fantasy Scoring Ranking
2009 ESPN	8th
2010 ESPN	16th
2010 CBSSports	15th
2011 CBS Sports	11th

How does this apply to us? Here is an example: I utilized numerous resources to rank players when preparing for my 2011 CBSSports league draft. But suppose I had relied entirely on CBSSports' preseason rankings (the ones on its fantasy website that correspond directly with one's league scoring system). Among the site's top 10 projected players at each position (60 players overall), those who accumulated fantasy point totals *outside* the top 10 at their position included the #1 ranked QB (Michael Vick), two of the top five ranked RBs (Chris Johnson and Jamaal Charles), three of the top five ranked WRs (Andre Johnson, Greg Jennings, and Hakeem Nicks), the #3 ranked TE (Dallas Clark), the #5 ranked K (Nate Kaeding), and two of the top five ranked DSTs (Jets and Eagles).

This does not make CBSSports a "bad" site. On the contrary, it has served me quite well over the years. But by 2011 I had understood that no single resource provides all of the answers. As shown in the breakdown above, had I drafted only top 10 ranked players at each position, on average they would have finished the season ranked only 15th in fantasy scoring at their respective position. In 2010 they would have averaged only a #14 positional ranking. As you know, that just won't cut it in fantasy football. Had I been seemingly lucky enough to draft only *top three* ranked players at each position, on average they would have finished the season ranked only 11th in fantasy scoring (15th in 2010) at their respective position—in other words, quite disappointing.

Conclusion: Don't trust all resources equally, and don't trust any single resource with your fantasy life. Anyone (and there are many of you) constructing a draft board based on a league website's predictions *before first analyzing its track record* is shooting himself in the foot before the race has begun. In the four examples above, ESPN's and CBSSports' fantasy ranking forecasts yielded results that would have hampered the title hopes of anyone basing roster decisions on such unreliable predictions.

Don't take the bait. Do your own research. Create your own draft list and rankings. And trust your *kick-ass* sensibilities.

CHAPTER 11

KICKING ASS ON DRAFT DAY

"Be formless, shapeless like water.
Now you put water into a cup, it becomes the cup. You pour water into a
bottle; it becomes the bottle. You put water into a teapot; it becomes the teapot.
Now water can flow, or creep or drip or crash! Be water, my friend."
– Bruce Lee

Imagine arriving at your fantasy draft without a care in the world. In place of customary fear is Zen-like calm. Look at your competitors' faces. What do you see? There is Jo-Jo with the first pick—the first overall pick for God's sake—frantically studying the latest edition of some two-bit draft guide magazine. And there is Willy Waddle, laughing at some ridiculous comment from the guy sitting beside him, as his right eye twitches while his left thumb and middle finger alt-tab through several generic fantasy ranking websites. The commissioner, Dumpy McGoo, fans through a stack of papers two inches high which he hurriedly printed at his office well after normal business hours, so no one would catch him.

Like an Olympian competing against neophytes still learning the rules, you are untouchable. You have trained harder, longer, and more effectively than everyone in that room combined. Your fantasy acumen is current, comprehensive, and creative. You eye victory not as a hope, but as a promise.

Fantasy football is 25% draft, 25% drops/adds, 25% starts/sits, and 25% luck. By controlling your fate with respect to the draft and regular season acquisitions, the curse of luck (injuries, suspensions, etc.) is mitigated—reduced to something that can be easily overcome. No pre-draft heavy lifting remains. What does remain is proper execution.

To kick ass on draft day, first you must be present. Don't fail to show because of some random family commitment, or because you just endured a gruesomely painful night that concluded with your spleen on the floor. No one will pick a better team for you than the one you will pick for yourself. Placing your roster's fate in a competitor's hands is like asking a roulette croupier to place your bets for you. If the hospital refuses to release you (because of that spleen problem), you should have planned ahead by organizing a bedside draft (and remember to request extended visiting hours). And do not even consider dialing into the draft. Who wants to keep shouting their picks so you can hear it clearly through the phone? You are only wasting time and pissing everyone off when you interrupt to ask, "Who were the last 14 players taken?" If you are this guy after all, then I cannot help you. Give this book to a co-worker with more self-respect.

At nearly every draft I have attended, at least one person is missing. The commissioner invariably asks the group, "Who wants to pick for [this loser]?" Then someone volunteers and proceeds to put in almost no thought in selecting the no-show's team. The result is a fantasy roster that looks much more like an expansion squad than a championship contender.

However, if you can be this volunteer, seize the opportunity. You will earn a little respect from the other league members, and especially from the absentee owner if he appreciates the half-decent team you assembled for him. Such integrity is not soon forgotten, particularly when proposing slightly lopsided trades (see Chapter 21). In addition, you can stack his team with players you would not want anyway, thus augmenting the possibility that slightly better talent will fall into your lap each round. But always remember—I repeat, *always remember*—to remove your Dirk hat when picking for someone else. I fell into this trap many years ago. As it is difficult to relay without breaking into tears, I will shield my heartache behind a lovely parable:

The Parable of the Good Samaritan Fantasy Drafter

A certain fantasy team owner named Eric had to leave town during the weekend of the annual fantasy draft, which would have stripped him of his team, which would have wounded his pride, and which would have left him bored for the next few months. He begged the other league owners to pick his team in his absence, so that he might have a team to return to.

And by chance there came a certain other fantasy team owner in the same league; and when he grasped the severity of the situation, he nevertheless rejected Eric's plea to pick his team. And likewise another owner saw him, and he too ignored Eric's entreaties.

But a certain Good Samaritan, when he was called by Eric, had compassion for him, and agreed to pick his team for him, and proceeded to pick an incredibly talented team—a team even more talented than the one he picked for himself.

Thinking I was buying a goodwill ticket to fantasy heaven, I agreed to pick for my longtime friend Eric. I don't recall why he was missing; he became a father the year before, so perhaps he had certain baby duties to which a guy like me could not relate. But whenever it was his turn, I stupidly picked as Dirk would: intelligently. For example, when making his fifth round selection, I handed him WR Randy Moss. Before you ask why Moss was still available at around the 55th pick, bear in mind that he was coming off his worst season ever: a relatively horrendous 553-yard, three-TD effort in 13 games that had shoved him off most drafters' early- and even middle-round radars. In fact, over his last three seasons Moss had averaged a pedestrian (for him) 775 receiving yards and eight TDs per year. Now 30 years old, the four-time All-Pro was a significant fantasy risk. But his recent move to the Patriots' high-powered offense increased the likelihood of a rebound year. So playing the role of a Good Samaritan and a *kick-ass* fantasologist, I drafted Moss for Eric's team, even though I probably would have snagged him for myself a few picks later.

It was not until Eric's powerhouse team beat me in Week 8 that I realized the extent of my self-inflicted damage. By season's end, the players I drafted for him included three of the top 15 overall fantasy scorers (an amazing concentration of talent for a 14-team league), including elite QB Drew Brees, the #1 scoring WR (Moss), the #1 scoring TE (Jason Witten), and the #2 DST (Patriots). My sense of decency led to fantasy ruin, and it continues to haunt me to this day.

The lesson is simple: **Your primary allegiance lies with your fantasy team**. Your family . . . friends . . . pet goldfish . . . they can fend for themselves. But your fantasy team is nothing without your total devotion. Whether drafting or making midseason roster moves, never compromise your capabilities. Everything you do is for the good of your team. Wussy attitudes don't lead to championships. *Kick-ass* attitudes do. Damn right.

So the next time your friend has to leave town or play with his baby or show some other blatant disregard for all that is holy in Fantasy Land, don't dare consider playing the Good Samaritan. Instead turn it to your advantage.

Once inside the draft room, find a comfortable seat. Do *not* sit off in a corner by yourself. Maintaining close proximity to competitors helps promote dialogue during the draft, followed by more valuable conversations during the season, which sometimes leads to favorable trades. It is also critically important that you not sit below others. Your research is gold; don't let opponents steal your gold. Sit at an even level or higher to help ensure that your fine-tuned player matrix and accompanying notes remain yours alone.

Next, initiate banter, engaging at least two people at a time. If you are a returning league member, casual conversation should be easy. If this is your first time with the group, show off your winning smile and charismatic voice while projecting humility. In addition to establishing social connections that might help you down the road, you are distracting others from last minute research. It's a win-win.

Along with the player matrix and notes, you also should have a couple of generic overall rankings and positional rankings from third-party sources. While these are not for you, they do serve three important functions:

(1) Use them to cover your real notes so that others cannot use them for their own gain.

(2) If some sorry sap asks to borrow a player rankings sheet, you have got him covered. This gracious move could help you during trade negotiations later. And since these rankings often are flawed, you sacrifice very little in return.

(3) A lot of people use similar rankings from a handful of online resources. Using these *dummy* ranking sheets, track who has been taken to help anticipate which guys might be drafted in the next few picks, thereby helping you plan your next move.

Picture a 12-round draft like it is a 12-round boxing match. You are trying to win each round—quite difficult when you are picking at or near the corners of a snake draft, but not far-fetched if you are prepared. Dutifully record every selection and eyeball how each will impact your next pick. As player after player is seized, focus on three core elements: *talent chasms*, *tier danglers*, and *runs*. By mastering these draft components, you will finish the night with the league's best crop of players . . . for any sport, every season.

At the end of the last chapter, I touched on talent chasms. You have seen these before: the division between two distinct tiers of players. For example, I am always pleasantly baffled when an opponent drafts the best second-tier RB right after worst first-tier RB has been taken, especially when a wide talent chasm exists between these two players. My reasoning might be obvious, but because you paid good money for this book, I will simplify it.

Imagine you have the sixth overall pick in a 10-team snake draft. After two QBs and three RBs go off the board, you select your top ranked WR, having already concluded that he will be more valuable to your team than your #3 projected QB or #4 projected RB. Remember, I am not telling you to draft your #1 projected WR any time you are handed the sixth overall pick. My example is based on hypothetical research you would have completed already, applying your player matrix, accompanying notes, and league scoring patterns to pinpoint the ideal player to select in each round.

During the next eight picks before your second selection, two more QBs, five more RBs, and one more WR are taken. Eight RBs have been drafted thus far. Your incomparable research has identified each position's talent chasms. Some days/weeks ago you found a talent chasm between your eighth and ninth ranked RBs. Essentially, the #8 RB's second round return on investment (ROI) is expected to be significantly greater than the #9 RB's second round ROI. Moreover, three other players remaining on the board—the #3 WR, #1 TE, and #1 DST—possess projected ROIs more closely aligned with RB 8's. Why settle for a significant drop-off when you can embrace a lateral selection? I will repeat this in bold because yes, it is *that* important: **Why settle for a significant drop-off when you can embrace a lateral selection?**

Too many drafters accept drop-offs without realizing it, while many others are resigned to their fate—sensing they are making a less-than-optimal pick, yet too fearful to buck convention. "Regardless of its fantasy upside, I just can't take a DST this early." Wrong answer. "If I don't land a QB in the first three rounds, everyone will laugh at me!" Pathetic. Stop playing it safe; play it *right*.

I hear the "QB in the first three rounds" comment all the time. Like lemmings, Jo-Jos expect everyone to follow the same rigid protocols: QB/RB in round one, RB/QB in round two, RB/WR in round three, etc. Dirk rejects preordained selection patterns. During prep for a 2011 draft, I identified three mid-level QBs poised for breakout seasons.

So rather than waste an early pick on a top-tier QB, I stacked my lineup with the projected second-ranked RB and two projected top 10 WRs. Meanwhile, in the first round four elite-level QBs went off the board. Two upper-tier QBs followed in the second frame, followed by two more in the third—including one of my three breakout QB candidates. That was the signal: it was time to act. On my next turn, I drafted my highest valued breakout option: Matthew Stafford.

Had I been unprepared, Stafford would have been ranked much lower on my draft sheet (as he was on everyone else's); after all, many "experts" placed him in the same camp as eventual waiver bait Josh Freeman and Sam Bradford. But based on thorough investigation, I predicted the third-year pro was drastically undervalued. And he did not disappoint, finishing the season ranked fourth in fantasy points—not merely among fellow QBs, but across the *entire league*. Not bad for a carefully calculated fourth round pick. "QB in the first three rounds"? Not always, my friend. Do your own research, and do it well, and the answers will come.

Now we will dig even deeper, so you can continue mind-melding with Dirk. We will assume that during draft prep you identified six tiers of players for each of six positions, equaling 36 tiers (or talent chasms) comprising 72 tier danglers. Referring to the following table, RB 8 and RB 9 are tier danglers, which are separated by a talent chasm. RBs 6, 7, and 8 have already been drafted:

Tier Danglers and Talent Chasms

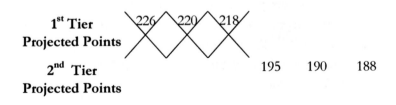

	RB 6	RB 7	RB 8	RB 9	RB 10	RB 11
1st Tier Projected Points	226	220	218			
2nd Tier Projected Points				195	190	188

Upper-tier danglers (e.g. RB 8) are players projected to accrue fantasy points more closely in line with slightly better players than with slightly worse players. *Lower*-tier danglers (e.g. RB 9) are the best of the next caliber of positional players, projected to accrue fantasy points more closely in line with their lower-tier neighbors than with the grouping of slightly better players. The following table presents another example:

Upper-Tier Danglers and Lower-Tier Danglers

	DST 1	DST 2	DST 3	DST 4	DST 5	DST 6	DST 7	DST 8
1st Tier Projected Points	211	204	193					
2nd Tier Projected Points				172	165	160	154	
3rd Tier Projected Points								129

As you can see, DSTs 4, 5, 6, and 7 clearly are below the top tier, which is comprised of DSTs 1, 2, and 3. The gap between DST 3 and DST 4 is a talent chasm if it is approximately as large as the gap between DST 4 and DST 7. DST 3 is an upper-tier dangler while DST 4 is a lower-tier dangler. Likewise, if the gap between DST 4 and DST 7 is roughly as large as the gap between DST 7 and DST 8, then the gap between DST 7 and DST 8 is another talent chasm, where DST 7 is an upper-tier dangler and DST 8 is a lower-tier dangler.

Lower-tier danglers hold value (more on this later), but timing is everything; selecting one too early means settling for a significant talent drop-off. On the other hand, an upper-tier dangler holds significant value when it is the most valuable option remaining on the board. Returning to our hypothetical second round selection, we bypass RB 9 because he is a lower-tier dangler; he might make a great third round pick ("timing is everything"), but remains overvalued in the second round. Remember those three guys—WR 3, TE 1, and DST 1—with projected ROIs akin to RB 8's (the player just taken)? Well, consult your player matrix and corresponding rankings. What do you see?

WR/TE/DST Draft Options

	WR 1	WR 2	WR 3	WR 4	WR 5	WR 6
1st Tier Projected Points	266	261	258	251		
2nd Tier Projected Points					225	219

	TE 1	TE 2	TE 3	TE 4	TE 5	TE 6
1st Tier Projected Points	244					
2nd Tier Projected Points		217	208			
3rd Tier Projected Points				173	168	165

	DST 1	DST 2	DST 3	DST 4	DST 5	DST 6
1st Tier Projected Points	211	204	193			
2nd Tier Projected Points				172	165	160

In this situation, Jo-Jo would scramble to find the next best QB or RB "just to keep up" with everyone else's picks, before the best ones "are all gone." But you know better. With the top WR under your belt, your best option for maximizing your weekly fantasy point production is drafting either your #3 ranked WR, #1 ranked TE, or #1 ranked DST. WR 3 is one of two top-tier athletes remaining at his position, while DST 1 is one of three. Yet TE 1 is the only player who is an upper-tier dangler. In addition, as the #1 ranked TE, he stands alone. Based on comprehensive research and analysis, you are confident that he has the best chance to score the most TE fantasy points. And although you have projected him 14 points below WR 3, the talent chasm between TE 1 and the next TE tier is far wider than the chasm between any other remaining first- and second-tier players. Depending on how many turns fall between your second and third round selections, it is possible that WR 4, and more likely that DST 3 (both upper-tier danglers), still will be available. But the risk of bypassing the ultimate upper-tier dangler—a #1 ranked positional player with high scoring potential—is too great.

So you grab TE 1. Two opponents laugh. A couple of others look down nervously at their cheat sheets as self-doubt creeps in. With picks upcoming, the anxious pair had planned to take an RB and WR, respectively. But after your selection, they fear missing out on the remaining top-tier TEs. So TE 2 and TE 3 come off the board. Congratulations: You have initiated a mini-run.

Most people think runs exist only in baseball, cricket, and pantyhose. But in fantasy drafts they are the stuff of legend. A potential run begins when you select a player from a position that has gone undrafted for some time (or upon a draft's initial selection of a position). If this move is closely followed by the selection of one or more players at that same position, you have initiated a run. In some ways it is rather similar to the stock market: An investor buys 100,000 shares of a lightly traded company. The move sets off a chain reaction, as other investors want to load up on the stock before it skyrockets. The prevailing thought is, "I don't want to get left out of this profitable opportunity."

A fantasy drafter like Jo-Jo thinks similarly: "If my opponents are now investing in TEs, I don't want to get left out." Jo-Jo believes that if three second-tier RBs are grabbed in succession in the third round, then he should grab the next best RB, too, regardless of this player's value compared to other available positional players. Poor Jo-Jo.

Your job as a *kick-ass* performer is to initiate as many runs as possible, inducing your competitors to seize the next best players at that position. So in the example above, you selected TE 1. Without interviewing them, we don't know if those two nervous guys picked the next best TEs because you initiated the pattern. But the fact is, they picked players you no longer need—the proverbial scraps off your dinner plate—while passing over players (RBs, WRs, etc.) that you might be targeting.

Let's advance to round four. In the 10 picks between your second and third selections, your opponents drafted two QBs, three RBs, three WRs, and the two aforementioned TEs. You really wanted that WR 4 to land in your lap, but no sweat. Your examination of existing danglers and potential runs was in full effect, leading to the prompt selection of DST 1. Several people laughed. Several more apprehensively poured through their cheat sheets, trying to make sense of it all. They know you know something. They just don't know what or how, because they have not prepared adequately for the draft . . . because they are not *kick-ass* players.

The next eight picks included two QBs, one RB, three WRs, and two DSTs (another mini-run you initiated!). You now have the #1 WR, #1 TE, and #1 DST in your back pocket. For simplicity, we will assume that each week you must start the following players: one QB, two RBs, two WRs, one TE, one K, one DST, and one "flex" player (an RB, WR, or TE). With this in mind, let's study your best fourth round options, keeping in mind that you no longer need a TE or DST, while a K would not yet provide sufficient value:

QB/RB/WR Draft Options

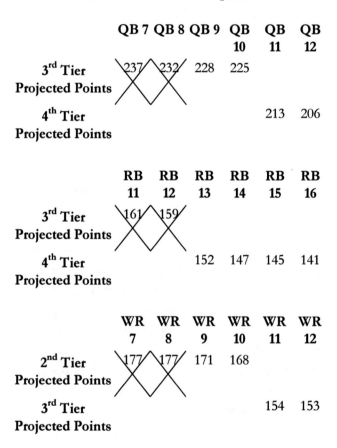

	QB 7	QB 8	QB 9	QB 10	QB 11	QB 12
3rd Tier Projected Points	237	232	228	225		
4th Tier Projected Points					213	206

	RB 11	RB 12	RB 13	RB 14	RB 15	RB 16
3rd Tier Projected Points	161	159				
4th Tier Projected Points			152	147	145	141

	WR 7	WR 8	WR 9	WR 10	WR 11	WR 12
2nd Tier Projected Points	177	177	171	168		
3rd Tier Projected Points					154	153

This dilemma should be familiar to the millions of Jo-Jos who have painfully endured fantasy drafts, and to the hundreds (soon to be thousands?) of Dirks who have thoroughly enjoyed dominating these same drafts. In this 10-team league, eight QBs are off the board. Unless someone wants to invest an early pick on a reserve #2 QB, QB 10 will be available for a while. So investing your fourth pick in QB 9 would be foolish, as you should be able to draft a comparable talent (QB 10) a few rounds later. In the meantime, there are higher impact players available at other positions.

Next you examine RB 13, a lower-tier dangler. Remember, timing is everything when drafting a lower-tier dangler. These players are the best of the next tier of talent. When selected too early, you are sacrificing fantasy value. When ignored for too long, they become very valuable commodities. The last RB lower-tier dangler we saw was RB 9, which you wisely bypassed in round two in order to claim TE 1 (an upper-tier dangler) with a much higher ROI. But RB 13 looks like a slightly better fourth round pick than RB 9 looked as a second round pick. Why? Only four RBs have been taken in the last 20+ selections. Since another 8-12 RBs will be drafted—and maybe more, depending on how each owner stocks his flex spot and reserves—selecting RB 13 might set off a run at that position. However, RBs 14, 15, and 16 are comparable to RB 13, while their projected points pale in comparison to the best QBs and WRs remaining.

So to summarize, in the rush to land a top-flight QB, eight have been taken. And since RBs are beloved in most fantasy drafts, this one is no exception, with 12 coming off the board in the first 34 picks. As a result, WRs are slightly underbought at this stage. So while WR 9 is not an upper-tier dangler, a mini-talent chasm exists after WR 10. "What's a 'mini' talent chasm?" you ask. You will find in draft preparation and execution that talent chasms usually are most robust between the first and second tiers, smaller between tiers two and three, and increasingly difficult to distinguish beyond that. This is because the NFL features a handful of elite players, a larger number of excellent players, and an even larger number of solid/"average" players. This is the nature of any sport, where greatness exists not only because it is objectively "great," but because it is so rare.

There is a mini-talent chasm between QB 10 and 11, RB 12 and 13, and WR 10 and 11. And as you see above, the chasm between WR 10 and WR 11 is larger than that of the other positions. Why? Because we are comparing second-tier WR talent, third-tier QBs, and fourth-tier RBs. WR 9 would give you the highest ROI at this point, and might even signal to others that it is time once again to pay attention to WRs (i.e. set off another run).

So you select WR 9. Sure enough, five of the next 10 picks are WRs. The others include a QB, two RBs, a TE, and a DST. Heading into your fifth selection, WRs are now *over*bought. Remember, never join the end of a run—nor in the middle of one if you can avoid it—as you will forfeit greater value found elsewhere. QB 10 is still waiting for a home. Someone might grab him as a backup at any time. But after surveying all near-term options, you conclude that using one of your later round picks on QB 11 or QB 12, if necessary, will make sense if you can add more positionally valuable talent during these next few rounds.

The draft has progressed organically, as you have re-evaluated and re-ranked potential targets depending on each opponent's pick. On another day in another draft room, someone else might have taken WR 1 before you, leaving QB 2 available, thereby shifting your entire approach going forward. You never know what will happen until it does. Until then, trust your matrix and keep your mind fluid; relax and ride the waves as they come.

While scanning your player matrix, here is what you see:

RB Draft Options

	RB 13	RB 14	RB 15	RB 16	RB 17	RB 18
4th Tier Projected Points	152	147	145	141	140	135

Are you excited that RB 15 is available in round five? In case you are wondering (and you should), your projection for RB 20 is 131 fantasy points. That means the top six remaining RBs are separated by only 14 points. Would you like to know where there is a greater differential among six players in the same position? Good, I thought you would:

K Draft Options

	K 1	K 2	K 3	K 4	K 5	K 6
1st Tier Projected Points	148	143	138			
2nd Tier Projected Points				131	120	115

In the two previous chapters we learned that some league point systems place several Ks among fantasy football's top 100 scorers by season's end, as well as how frequently the #1 scoring K accumulates more fantasy points than the #15 scoring RB. In the above table, you have projected K 1 to amass 33 more points than K 6—a much larger differential than that found between RBs 15 and 20. K 1 also is projected to earn more fantasy points than RB 15. I realize you still don't have an RB or a QB. "This is madness," you say, doing your best Jo-Jo impression. But the only madness I see is owners choosing lesser talent at supposed "premier" positions rather than greater talent at less glamorous positions.

But there is one option you might not have considered: grabbing DST 5 or 6, choosing whichever one's schedule aligns best with your DST 1's schedule:

DST Draft Options

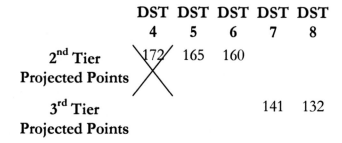

	DST 4	DST 5	DST 6	DST 7	DST 8
2nd Tier Projected Points	172	165	160		
3rd Tier Projected Points				141	132

For example, if DST 1 has three very tough matchups this season and DST 6 (an upper-tier dangler) has a much easier matchup in each of those weeks, you could take a flier on DST 6, knowing it probably will help you for three weeks (plus DST 1's bye week). In addition, it could serve as terrific trade bait for an owner desperately seeking an upgrade from the 10th or 11th best DST. DST 6 offers fourth round value at a fifth round price. You have far more to gain than to lose by making this selection.

I have now presented a few hypothetical rounds to help you understand the *kick-ass* approach required for success, so that you can dominate the draft and move closer to the title. As the rounds continue, you will always know precisely which player will give you the highest ROI at any moment. When it is your turn, you will pick with confidence. And when it is not your turn (as you will learn later), you still possess resources for improving your team.

You cannot wait until later? Then I will give you a sampling. Suppose we are back in round five. You are still deciding between RB 15, K 1, and DST 6. Unless another Dirk is lurking in the draft room, there is a very good chance no one will take K 1 before your sixth pick, a decent chance no one will take DST 6, and almost no chance RB 15 will be available. In this situation, you might wish to trade down, offering someone your current and following pick (fifth and sixth round) in exchange for his fifth and sixth rounders.

Let's say your potential trade partner selects three spots after you in round five. If he is worried that a player he desperately wants will be gone before his next turn arrives, then both of you have something to gain by trading. With your new next pick (his old fifth rounder), you can select whichever player (K 1, DST 6, or RB 15) remains. And now armed with his early sixth rounder (pick #52) instead of your old sixth rounder (pick #55), you are in a better position to land one of your two other targets.

The reverse approach also can help you maximize your roster value. A few years ago, noticing an opponent struggling to make his fifth round selection, I (trading three spots after him that round) offered my fifth and sixth frame picks in exchange for his immediate selection and sixth frame pick. On paper it was a virtual wash. And since he clearly was choosing among at least two players, presumably he could afford to defer his selection by three spots without sacrificing talent, and in the process improve his selection prospects in the following round six.

Little did he know that I had already targeted the Bears as my #1 DST and was waiting for the best opportunity to strike. In my CBSSports league, almost no one takes a DST until around the 70th or 80th overall pick. At the time, we were approaching pick #60. Eyeing his prolonged deliberation and concerned that he might start a run on DSTs, I made the offer. He promptly declined with a quick shake of his head. But after taking another minute to weigh options, he relented.

I immediately grabbed the Bears DST, which finished that season with the sixth most fantasy points *overall*. And which player did my trade partner take three picks later? The Buccaneers DST, which tied for 157th place among fantasy scorers that year. I claimed a prized target while simultaneously kick-starting a mini-run on DSTs, and rode the Bears and four other top 30 overall scorers to an easy title. Meanwhile, my opponent dropped the Bucs after Week 3.

That is how you draft to win.

The Huddle

As stated in the previous *Huddle*, I have tracked preseason fantasy predictions from ESPN (2009 and 2010 seasons) and CBSSports (2010 and 2011 seasons) to determine how accurate they are. I am a big fan of both sites' news reporting and fantasy game platforms. However, being a *kick-ass* manager, I wanted to quantify the degree to which I should incorporate their rankings into my initial fantasy decisions each season.

Based on their top 10 preseason rankings at each position (QB, RB, WR, TE, K, and DST), how many players (out of 60 overall) finished the season in the top 10 in fantasy scoring at their position?

Preseason Top 10 Predictions:
Top 10 Positional Fantasy Scoring Accuracy (Season)

	Top 10 Fantasy Scorers	Percentage Correct
2009 ESPN	28 out of 60	47%
2010 ESPN	35 out of 60	58%
2010 CBSSports	34 out of 60	57%
2011 CBS Sports	28 out of 60	47%

Conclusion: Building upon our previous *Huddle*, neither ESPN's nor CBSSports' website rankings system consistently predicted which players would finish in the top 10 at each position. If you make draft decisions and regular season roster moves based on any website's preseason rankings *that you have not first analyzed carefully*, don't be surprised by disappointing results. That might suffice for Jo-Jo, but Dirk sees no reason to take such unnecessary risks. Through *kick-ass* research, you can learn how to make considerably more accurate ranking predictions than any website.

CHAPTER 12

POST-DRAFT RESEARCH
(YOU'RE NOT DONE YET)

"One never notices what has been done;
one can only see what remains to be done."
– Marie Curie

You step through your front door after a four-hour draft so empowering, so exhilarating, so triumphant that all you want to do is read to your children, call your dear old mama, and sleep with your wife.

With the season still on the line? Are you nuts? You should know by now that Dirk never rests until victory is secured.

Immediately after drafting in a 14-team league in 2010, I remained on my computer and read that only moments earlier, the Texans had placed RB Ben Tate, on IR (injured reserve). Only a few hours earlier he was in strong contention for Houston's lead back role. Now one week into the preseason, such honors would be decided by a two-man battle between third-year RB Steve Slaton and little-known second-year RB Arian Foster.

Neither Slaton nor Foster had been drafted in our league that night; with only 10 roster spots on each team, there were plenty of seemingly better RB options at the time. Who wants to take a chance on a potentially third-string RB when there are so many second-stringers and dual time-sharers left on the board? However, the loss of Tate changed this dynamic completely. My fantasy league accepted pickups and drops at any time during the preseason. So unlike my pre-draft analysis, this latest research was extraordinarily time-sensitive; as soon as other league members heard about Tate's fate, Slaton and/or Foster could be snatched in a matter of seconds.

I utilized my best Web news resources and cross-checked these findings with what Houston-area sports analysts were saying. I analyzed illuminating statistical data showing that, after a stellar rookie campaign, Slaton's production dropped off in his sophomore season, as he eventually shared RB duties with several teammates. One of these players, Arian Foster, ran for 216 yards and three TDs over the last two games of the 2009 season.

Despite Foster's promising end-of-year showing, it took about 20 minutes to verify his preseason edge over Slaton. So I took a calculated risk, adding Foster to my roster and dropping my #4 WR, Braylon Edwards. Edwards went on to score 135 fantasy points in 2010—good for 20th among WRs. Not too shabby for an underrated receiver I landed late in the draft. Too bad I had to let him go. Alas, the curse of that league's short bench, where only two reserves are permitted.

And what about that virtual unknown named Arian Foster who, heading into our early preseason draft was among dozens of RBs with scant chance of achieving fantasy relevance? That season he scored 290 fantasy points—the second most *among all players*. That, my friends, is why post-draft research is an essential ingredient in Dirk's fantasy recipe. You can work your butt off preparing for the draft. But if you abandon that *kick-ass* attitude for even one moment, you will miss numerous roster-enhancing opportunities.

Now let's hear from Jo-Jo:

Me: *"Jo-Jo, what is your post-draft ritual?"*

Jo-Jo: "The bathroom. After scarfing down all those nachos and warm beer at the draft, I'm absolutely bursting when I get home."

Me: "What else do you do?"

Jo-Jo: "There's no time for anything else. By the time I'm finished, it's time for bed."

Me: "Is it worth it?"

Jo-Jo: "Are you kidding? After about an hour-and-a-half, I feel like a new man."

Me: "No, I mean, is it worth it to come home and ignore your fantasy obligations?"

Jo-Jo [pauses]: "It's nap time."

Fantasy sports is a friendless occupation, dear readers. It is you against the world. When Vincent Price fought against fairly tame zombie-like creatures in *The Last Man on Earth,* and seven years later Charlton Heston engaged nerve-rattling, post-biological warfare mutants in *The Omega Man,* and decades later Will Smith battled bat-shit-scary zombies in *I Am Legend,* we did not observe them taking poo breaks. They did not risk life and limb to reach a hell-hole grocery store across town to secure an unexpired jar of organic guacamole for that night's Mexican-themed dinner-for-one. They were too busy combating the freakin' undead. From awaking at dawn to closing one eye at dusk while the other eye stood watch, these bad-asses never rested. And neither should you. Just replace "zombie conflict" with "fantasy research."

Remember the player matrix you spent several hundred hours assembling? This little baby will continue feeding your team right into the playoffs and on to victory. As soon as you get home, update your matrix to reflect draft results. Who was taken? Who remains? Who are your targets?

You might notice that no one drafted seven WRs listed as #2 on their respective team's depth chart. Many #2 WRs finish the season with respectable fantasy numbers. And many available #2 WRs likely qualify as *mediocre* performers with the potential to shine in certain weeks. Do you recall my discussion on mediocrity in Chapter 3? Does **Kick-Ass Rule #4** ring a bell? "Mediocre players are the difference makers." Many of your matrix's 150-300 undrafted players (depending on the number of owners and roster spots in your league) will enjoy at least one terrific fantasy performance this season. Some will enjoy sizable fantasy production in several games. And as we witness every season in every league, a handful will become fantasy studs.

Treat these 150-300 undrafted players like newborn octuplets: track their every move and don't let them out of your sight. When you learn new information about a player, determine whether it is newsworthy enough to reorder him in the matrix. Perhaps you read that a team is grooming its rookie #2 TE to replace the #1 TE sometime this season. Well hell, this is prime intelligence, particularly if you are weak at the TE slot. If your bench is deep enough, and that rookie is promising enough, you might make room for him at this instant. At the very least he should remain on your radar, with the goal of adding him before another league owner catches wind of his fantasy scoring potential.

Speaking of competition, expect each opponent to shed about 10%-30% of their drafted team by season's end.

Some drops are due to injury or suspension, while others result from athletes playing worse than expected. But occasionally owners lose patience with an underperforming talent that you believe still possesses high value. By tracking others' current players, you can learn more than they know, and can parlay that familiarity into roster upgrades.

For example, in one of my 2011 leagues, undrafted rookie WR A.J. Green was one of many free agents I tracked after the draft. In the preseason, CBSSports projected him as the 46th highest scoring fantasy WR, which, as you know by now, hardly influenced my view of his potential. The Bengals entered the season without their starting QB and top two WRs from 2010. A rookie QB was stepping into an offense that included several relatively unproven WRs with NFL experience, as well as Green, who many experts believed could become a fantasy stud . . . in 2012 or '13. It was believed that he would endure too many ups and downs this year to contribute consistently.

However, my pre-draft research had demonstrated that he was a certifiable candidate for fantasy success *this season*. By tracking him early, I was prepared to pounce after Week 2. Serving as my #2 WR on a team that featured fantasy studs like Arian Foster, Matthew Stafford, and Greg Jennings, Green accrued a solid 58 fantasy points in five games.

My roster was now set, right? Of course not. Because throughout the preseason and regular season, I also tracked other teams' players, especially underperformers. Roddy White was one of those players. The perennial fantasy star had racked up only 61 fantasy points in his first seven games and was coming off a Week 8 bye. After carrying White patiently for nearly half a season, a league opponent was finally ready to part ways. Yet whom could I hand over in return? Green had scored more fantasy points than White through eight weeks. But I observed that White had earned about 50% more targets per game than Green, and I was fairly certain that his many extra opportunities eventually would lead to bigger production during the season's critical second half.

Meanwhile, with less than five receptions per contest, Green had benefited almost entirely from one or two big plays per contest. The rookie's feast-or-famine situation had cooked up many feasts so far, making him appear better on paper than White. But beyond the stats lay the risk that at least this season, in his team's present system, Green had reached his fantasy ceiling, while White's ceiling lay much higher.

So I swapped Green for White because I understood White's greater potential—not by hunches or guesses, but by research that began before the draft and continued immediately following the draft. The result: For his new team, Green amassed 72 points (nine points per game and 25th most among WRs during the season's second half), while for my team, White netted 123 points (13.7 points per game and tied for third among WRs during the season's second half). Starting with nothing, I developed enough expertise to land two successive WR upgrades—first through the waiver process (Green), and then through a trade (White). This process began before the draft and continued as soon as I returned home.

That is why we never stop researching.

Some leagues add a roster spot for players on IR. I am continually shocked how often my opponents fail to fill this position. Such a sad waste. *Always* plug your IR spot with the injured player who is most likely to score the most fantasy points, particularly during your league playoffs—or if you compete in a keeper league, perhaps someone with the highest fantasy point potential next season. It sounds obvious, but not to Jo-Jo. If a star player is out until "at least Week 11," and if that guy (when he returns) is more likely to contribute more fantasy points than any other IR guy, then pick him up immediately. Concerned that he might help you for nothing more than your league playoffs? Boo-hoo. What a shame. Concerned he will not be fully healed? You have nothing to lose. Add him to your roster, track his rehab progress, and use him as trade bait or for a late-season fantasy production boost. And if a better IR candidate comes along, simply upgrade.

Don't limit post-draft work merely to the Internet. Relying on stats alone is a two-dimensional solution to a three-dimensional challenge. Adjust your waking life so it aligns with the NFL's preseason television schedule. Fantasy football TV shows are relatively worthless if you have embraced due diligence, as these programs essentially rehash what you know. However, *watching* football games (as you will see in Chapter 15) is critical to any *kick-ass* regimen.

In addition, initiate a daily routine of reading fantasy football news/blogs (stop panicking; these are the ones you bookmarked already, per Chapter 9). Morning, afternoon, and evening are perfect times to brush up on the latest information. And don't forget to program news alerts into your mobile device(s), ensuring that all fantasy news nuggets reach you before any opponent hears about them.

Remember that while several players drafted in your league will fall well short of expectations, many *undrafted* athletes will kick ass at some point(s) during the season. Any number of frees agents could be your tickets to fantasy stardom. Find them before your opponents do.

The Huddle

Among players who scored the most fantasy points at their position each week, how frequently did ESPN and CBSSports rank them in the top 10 at their position that week?

Weekly #1 Positional Fantasy Scorers:
Weekly Top 10 Positional Ranking Frequency

	QB	RB	WR	TE	K	DST	% Correct
ESPN 2009	9	11	9	9	6	7	**50.0%**
ESPN 2010	9	7	7	12	11	8	**52.9%**
CBSSports 2010	10	8	6	10	7	9	**49.0%**
CBSSports 2011	13	10	7	12	6	11	**57.8%**
% Correct	**60.3%**	**52.9%**	**42.6%**	**63.2%**	**44.1%**	**51.5%**	**52.5%**

Among players who scored the second most fantasy points at their position each week, how frequently did ESPN and CBSSports rank them in the top 10 at their position that week?

Weekly #2 Positional Fantasy Scorers:
Weekly Top 10 Positional Ranking Frequency

	QB	RB	WR	TE	K	DST	% Correct
ESPN 2009	7	11	6	7	12	11	**52.9%**
ESPN 2010	11	8	7	9	5	10	**49.0%**
CBSSports 2010	10	9	6	10	7	9	**50.0%**
CBSSports 2011	10	11	5	9	13	5	**52.0%**
% Correct	**55.9%**	**57.4%**	**35.3%**	**51.5%**	**54.4%**	**51.5%**	**51.0%**

And among players who scored the third most fantasy points at their position each week, how frequently did ESPN and CBSSports rank them in the top 10 at their position that week?

Weekly #3 Positional Fantasy Scorers: Weekly Top 10 Positional Ranking Frequency

	QB	RB	WR	TE	K	DST	% Correct
ESPN 2009	10	7	4	8	5	10	**43.1%**
ESPN 2010	12	12	3	13	6	6	**51.0%**
CBSSports 2010	8	9	5	10	9	5	**45.1%**
CBSSports 2011	15	7	5	9	11	10	**55.9%**
% Correct	**66.2%**	**51.5%**	**25.0%**	**58.8%**	**45.6%**	**45.6%**	**48.8%**

Conclusion: Among each week's top three fantasy point scorers at each position (18 players total), ESPN accurately ranked them in its weekly top 10 slightly below 50% of the time over two combined seasons, while CBSSports accurately ranked them a little above 51.5% of the time over two combined seasons. WRs were by far the most difficult position to predict, while QBs were the easiest, followed by TEs.

Building on earlier warnings, don't trust weekly rankings that frequently exclude the week's leading fantasy scorers at each position. Many eventual top performers are either free agents or riding a competitor's bench. Do your homework: identify them, acquire them, and start them based on accumulated knowledge.

CHAPTER 13

HOW'S MY MONEY DOING?
(KEEPING TABS ON THE POT)

"Money money money money, money."
– The O'Jays

Earlier I mentioned the commissioner who prematurely folded our computerized fantasy baseball league and pocketed our entry fees. That cash went a long way toward buying his still-beloved Paul Anka records. Fortunately the life lesson I learned back then cost me  only five dollars. But in your fantasy league, the stakes probably are higher. So heed this warning: Take extra precautions to ensure that everyone's hard-earned entry fees will greet you on the other side of victory.

First, never pay cash unless the commissioner gives you a signed and notarized letter in return. Make sure it is printed on the fantasy league's letterhead. (No fantasy league letterhead? Tell the commissioner to get off his ass and do his job.) Feel free to send him this template, which is legally bulletproof.*

* Warning: might not be legally bulletproof

Date: [Date]

To: [Your name]

(Also add *city and date of birth,* ensuring that no one else with your name stakes claim to your money. If your city and date of birth are somewhat common [e.g. "New York City" and "January in the '70s" {assuming you don't know your birthday}], then you might add another option like *favorite color.* Then choose an unusual favorite color [e.g. "sickly orange"]. Then draft a second signed and notarized letter declaring that your favorite color is sickly orange. An earlier draft of this book included language for this second letter, but my publisher said it was excessive.)

Re: Fantasy Football Payment for [Name of league, name of commissioner, and city and date of birth of commissioner] (Don't you dare skip ahead. I have watched people lose hundreds of dollars—hundreds—by omitting this information. Shut up and read.)

Your fingerprints	Commissioner's fingerprints

I, [commissioner's name], as identified above, do solemnly swear that [your name], as identified above, has submitted to me, [commissioner's name], as identified above, $[amount of cash] as payment for entry into [name of league, year], as identified above, for which I, [commissioner's name], as identified above, am serving as commissioner.

(If these pages become separated, the "identified above" language protects you. What if the commissioner gets a divorce and loses page two in the settlement? Then suppose a fire partially chars page two, and the commissioner's ex-wife sells the rest of it to a fantasy museum? What then? See where I am going with this? Cover your bases. And stop complaining: We are almost done.)

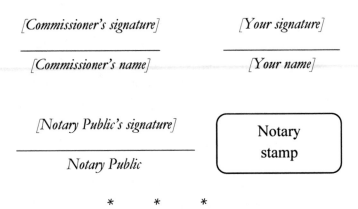

[Commissioner's signature]   *[Your signature]*
_____   _____
[Commissioner's name]   *[Your name]*

[Notary Public's signature]   Notary
_____   stamp
Notary Public

*　　*　　*

Of course, each league member will have already signed a separate document outlining the league's rules, including when and how the prize money is distributed. The template above simply protects you against an ill-intentioned, oft-forgetful, or half-drunken commissioner who otherwise would not record your payment.

PayPal payments, credit card payments, personal checks, or game show checks are fine methods to use. Just be sure you have paper and electronic trails to reference later in case the commissioner tries to make you pay twice. I prefer to use my wife's credit card to prove what a feminist I am.

Next come the weekly phone calls, when you verify from the commissioner that he still is in possession of the prize money. Although known for their stoic temperance and firm handshakes, some commissioners are weasels who "invest" prize money in "video cameras" for the production of "home erotica." They hope that by marketing seemingly discreet dalliances of a middle-aged married couple, they will recoup their finances and invest their profits in sexy undergarment shops.

But you are smarter than the commissioner, by simple measure that you have elected not to become one. In addition to weekly calls, visit the commissioner's home every other week—unannounced—to see the money for yourself. If the commissioner cannot produce the prize payout, then you are legally obligated to take his flat-screen TV or some other easily transportable device of at least twice the value of your league entry payment. (It is a good idea to get this in writing first so you are "on the same page" and not "charged with second-degree theft").

If the commissioner does not have the money at home, demand that he lead you to it, whether it is stored in a bank vault, buried in the back yard, or crumpled in his uncle's clenched fist at the racetrack. Once there, photograph the stash and e-mail the picture to the other league members; think of this last step as a public service. Some people donate thousands of dollars each year to charities. Others volunteer hundreds of hours for philanthropic causes. *Kick-ass* fantasy players e-mail prize money photos to competitors.

Follow this comprehensive approach with the same vigor and dedication as you would any fantasy-related responsibility, so that after winning the championship, you need not wonder, "Will I receive what I have rightfully earned?" By adopting a few simple steps, you can sleep soundly knowing that your future bounty softly calls your name and patiently awaits your firm hands and deep pockets.

The Huddle

The previous *Huddle* addressed how frequently each week's top performers were included in ESPN's and CBSSports' top 10 rankings. Now let's reverse course: Among ESPN's and CBSSports' weekly #1 picks at each position, what percentage of players finished among the top 10 in fantasy scoring at their position that week. In other words, rather than calculating the frequency of top performers' inclusion in pregame rankings, let's analyze the weekly performance of these websites' top predictions.

Weekly #1 Picks:
Weekly Top 10 Positional Fantasy Scoring Frequency

	QB	RB	WR	TE	K	DST	% Correct
ESPN 2009	9	9	5	13	7	11	**52.9%**
ESPN 2010	9	10	2	11	5	9	**45.1%**
CBSSports 2010	9	10	4	11	7	9	**49.0%**
CBSSports 2011	13	12	8	9	4	11	**55.9%**
% Correct	**58.8%**	**60.3%**	**27.9%**	**64.7%**	**33.8%**	**58.8%**	**50.7%**

Furthermore, what percentage of ESPN's and CBSSports' weekly #2 picks at each position finished among the top 10 in fantasy scoring at their position that week?

Weekly #2 Picks:
Weekly Top 10 Positional Fantasy Scoring Frequency

	QB	RB	WR	TE	K	DST	% Correct
ESPN 2009	9	8	6	10	3	8	**43.1%**
ESPN 2010	9	6	8	9	5	11	**47.1%**
CBSSports 2010	7	6	5	9	6	10	**42.2%**
CBSSports 2011	14	10	4	9	12	8	**55.9%**
% Correct	**57.4%**	**44.1%**	**33.8%**	**54.4%**	**38.2%**	**54.4%**	**47.1%**

Finally, what percentage of ESPN's and CBSSports' weekly #3 picks finished among the top 10 in fantasy scoring at their position that week?

Weekly #3 Picks:
Weekly Top 10 Positional Fantasy Scoring Frequency

	QB	RB	WR	TE	K	DST	% Correct
ESPN 2009	10	9	3	12	4	13	50.0%
ESPN 2010	7	7	6	7	7	5	38.2%
CBSSports 2010	13	6	4	8	8	7	45.1%
CBSSports 2011	13	9	6	11	7	10	54.9%
% Correct	63.2%	45.6%	27.9%	55.9%	38.2%	51.5%	47.1%

Conclusion: A combined 48.3% of the time, these two sites' top three picks (at each position) ranked among that week's top 10 positional scorers. While #1 picks were accurate just under 51% of the time, #2 and #3 picks were accurate just over 47% of the time. CBSSports' cumulative accuracy hovered just above 50%, while ESPN's was just over 46%.

We have already covered the challenges many websites face when attempting to assign predictive rankings, and these latest results reinforce the point. Imagine your luck if *each* of your weekly starters during these analyzed seasons had been ranked among the top three weekly players at each position by ESPN or CBSSports. You would have gone undefeated, right? Who *wouldn't* embrace the luxury of starting each week's premier projected talent?

Yet based on our analyzed results, a majority (combining top-, second-, and third-ranked picks) of these supposed fantasy studs would have finished the week outside the top 10 in fantasy scoring at their respective position. As a result, even by possessing each week's highest projected fantasy production, victory would have been far from guaranteed.

The most interesting angle from these numbers is that WRs once again were the most difficult position to predict, followed by Ks. And again, QBs were the easiest position to predict, followed closely by TEs. The challenge of predicting WR success is due, in all likelihood, to the large number of WRs who are viable fantasy contributors each week. Unlike the five other positional players, as many as 65-75 WRs enter each non-bye week as a potentially relevant fantasy entity, and roughly 40-50 produce fantasy points ranging from half-decent (e.g. five catches for 70 yards) to exceptional (e.g. 10 catches for 120 yards and two TDs).

We might conclude, therefore, that while you should view any third-party ranking system with suspicion until properly vetted, consistently predicting WR performance with relative accuracy might be too difficult a task for any website, as the player pool is too large and unwieldy for anyone but Dirk to master.

PART III

THE REGULAR SEASON

Famous Days in Fantasy Football History

October 28, 1962

The New York Giants' Y.A. Tittle passes for 505 yards and seven touchdowns, leading accountant Jimmy Sampson's **Lawrence Welkathons** to a 105-97 victory over typist Julia Fontaine's **Andy Warhol of Famers.**

The loss drops Ms. Fontaine's record to 2-6, prompting her to mail a first-class letter to her league's commissioner announcing that this would be her final season.

CHAPTER 14

ROSTER AND LINEUP DECISIONS:
PREGAME DOS AND DON'TS

"You don't concentrate on risks. You concentrate on results.
No risk is too great to prevent the necessary job from getting done."
– Chuck Yeager

Congratulations! You have reached the regular season with nary a bruise, except perhaps to your ego, as you realize just how awful a fantasy player you have been all these years. I have explained much about what the fantasy universe requires from you to win. If you do not yet understand the importance of disciplined research and analysis, don't expect to grasp it during the season. If you do not yet possess a cadre of news resources feeding you facts and figures minute by minute, don't expect to start now. If you have not warned your family to stay away during fantasy football season, don't be surprised if all hell breaks loose by Week 4.

What you are today is what you endeavored to become in July and August. If you embody the essence of Dirk (including his winning scent) by Week 1, then you are well on your way to the title.

Next you will learn how to augment your *kick-ass* behavior across all facets of managing your fantasy team during the regular season. One poorly planned date night (read: any night), ill-conceived work commitment ("Sure, Mr. Jenkins, I'll stay late."), or prolonged and debilitating illness (i.e. stale burrito) threatens to undo everything you have worked toward. The preseason revealed whether you have what it takes. A properly executed regular season will bestow upon you that long sought after doctorate in fantasology.

Let's examine a typical Sunday, during which a majority of NFL games are played. If you are like me (and you'd better be by now), game days should not be "fun." But few things in life are more rewarding when handled with the sheer artistry of a fantasy wizard. Game days require more investment of your time and resources than anything you encounter during the week. Sundays, in particular, are more physically demanding than the Boston Marathon, more mentally taxing than the bar exam, and more spiritually arousing than a Phish concert.

Your Sunday begins at 5:00 a.m. EST (suck it up, West Coasters) with the rapid-fire downing of four raw eggs (à la Rocky) and vomiting at least three of them (à la me). Then hit the street for a morning jog to clear your head and tighten your butt; a flabby ass simply will not stand up to the rigors of sitting on a couch for 12 hours. This run should mark the only period when you are outside your house without an Internet device. Focus on positive thinking. Contemplate your own fantasy greatness. No one can touch you. And as your wife attests, no one should, especially out on the street at 5:00 a.m.

When you return an hour later, exhausted and refreshed, let the fantasy world back in. While my favorite sports talk radio program blares in the background, I enjoy a hot 30-minute shower to stimulate the senses. Also I smell quite rank after 12 hours in front of the tube, simmering in sweat and farts. So consider this step a pre-emptive measure to ward off those anticipated family complaints:

> **Wife and Kids:** *"Honey/Dad, you smell like that thing in our basement—the thing we're not supposed to touch."*

> **Me:** *"And where were you earlier when I was the embodiment of dandelions and cardamom?"*

Invariably this conversation will end in victory when your family must vacate the room after inhaling too many airborne toxins. Since you have already acquired immunity to such pollutants (thanks to countless game days), the room is now your private sanctuary, in which your TV is the altar and your laptop is scripture.

But I am getting ahead of myself. It is still only 6:30 a.m. If you have not done so previously, take a few moments to Facebook friend your players and targets and start following them on Twitter to track their latest doings. Then send a simple game day message to each of your players, imploring them to rack up a record number of fantasy points. If you took care of this before Week 1, e-mail them again on Sunday morning of Week 2 to (a) thank them for last week's performance, (b) announce that it temporarily saved your marriage, and (c) request an encore performance to help cure your narcolepsy. Rinse and repeat until you are crowned champion.

Despite assumptions to the contrary, *kick-ass* fantasy football and religious practice are not mutually exclusive; your weekly spiritual activities need not be compromised. Simply bring an Internet-ready device to track the latest football news while simultaneously serving your Lord. If your church/temple/mosque does not have Internet access, place a hand-written request on the collection plate or in the suggestions box, and in the meantime bring plenty of printed reading material. When praying, beg for fortune to shine its glorious light upon your players. If meditation is more your thing, rather than concentrate on breathing, focus on what must be going through each of your player's minds. Then unite your karma with theirs, instilling in them a never-quit attitude for today's matchup. As for other teams' players, use your influence over the universe to instill fear in their hearts.

By 9:00 a.m. your daily non-fantasy responsibilities should be fulfilled. But I have often discovered that others' so-called "emergencies" arise when we least expect or want them to, such as when the kids are hungry and are too small to reach the breakfast cereal (though that is why God invented stools), or when they refuse to finish their (formerly your) household chores. In addition, it is always possible that your girlfriend/wife will demand attention, conveniently forgetting that this is, after all, football season.

Such crises are handled deftly by Dirks, so listen carefully. Your primary obligation to fantasy football should not weaken your family unit. On the contrary, it should transform your family such that each member grows more independent, and thus more capable of overcoming her/his own challenges. So give your diminutive children plywood and a saw and encourage them to learn how to construct stilts. For household chores like lawn care, "mow time" becomes "go time"; bring your mobile device and read while you glide across the grass. As for your loving partner, encourage her to seek solace from her female friends, particularly if they are competitors in your league (distract the opposition).

After solving these family emergencies by 9:05 a.m. you are ready to dig in for the day. Begin by reading the latest entries on all bookmarked websites. This exercise has been a frequent activity since the preseason (or even earlier), and by now has been incorporated into your daily/nightly routine. However, such research takes on a new level of importance with games around the corner.

In 2007 I visited a friend in Atlanta. Competing in different leagues, we could watch Sunday's games without the risk of one of us beating up the other. During my standard pregame research routine, I learned 15 minutes before the opening kickoff that his starting TE was a last-minute scratch. "Crap," he said after I told him the news. "Who should I play?" Rather than belabor the point that he clearly had not read my last blog post in which I tagged Chris Cooley as that week's #1 undervalued TE, I quickly guided him through the lineup change. About 45 minutes later, Cooley scored a TD. It was that simple.

So to recap, 15 minutes before kickoff my friend was unprepared to replace his injured starter. Because of thorough research completed throughout the week, I was. Dirks of the world are always prepared to overcome even worst-case scenarios like last-minute injuries.

But these issues are not always cut-and-dried. Suppose your starting QB recently was slapped with a "questionable" tag due to bruised ribs. Such players frequently remain in limbo until a couple of hours (and sometimes a couple of minutes) before the opening kick. Hopefully you have already mitigated the situation by acquiring a high-upside QB to fill in, if needed.

However, suppose this injury was first announced at 9:00 a.m. EST. If your league permits roster changes this late in the week, you are fantasologically obligated to research all available options quickly and add the free agent QB most likely to score the most fantasy points that week. In addition, you must verify by any means possible whether your #1 QB will be cleared to play (and will be capable of producing as expected).

Maximizing fantasy points requires a "leave no stone unturned" mentality. At a party in late 1999 I suggested to some friends that we launch a fantasy NCAA basketball league. Drawing from the 10 athletic conferences that corresponded with our respective alma maters, we drafted one player from each conference. At the time I was working 15 hours per day, seven days per week on a presidential campaign (I had not yet adopted the "nothing matters more than fantasy sports" doctrine). And yet I carved out a few minutes each day to track the performance of my players and free agent targets.

James Madison University's Jabari Outzz was my Colonial Athletic Conference pick. But he missed the first two games with an injury. Back then the Internet held a fraction of the seemingly limitless sports news it possesses now—particularly with respect to college basketball and certainly when it came to fantasy news. With no information about Outzz's status for his next game against East Tennessee State University, and preferring not to bench such a potentially high-impact player, I sought an answer directly from the source; I called JMU's Athletic department:

JMU Athletic Department Rep.:
"Hello, JMU Athletics."

Me: *"Hello, I'm a huge JMU fan, and Jabari Outzz is my favorite player."*

JMU Athletic Department Rep.:
"Well, that's great to hear."

Me: *"I really want to come to the next game and watch Jabari do his thing. Do you think he'll be able to suit up?"*

JMU Athletic Department Rep.:
"Oh, don't worry. He'll be fine for the next game."

Mission accomplished. Indeed, Outtz played in the next game and in every other game that season, finishing with the best per-game stats of his college career. Earning Colonial Athletic Conference First Team honors, he finished fourth in the CAA in points, third in assists, third in three-point field goals, and third in free throw percentage—all categories in which my fantasy league competed. Needless to say, I ran away with the fantasy title.

The lesson should be obvious: Do whatever it takes to win, and don't take "no" for an answer. Your weekly lineup should be nearly bulletproof—that is, it should contain players who have the highest probability of success. There were other players available in my college basketball league, and some might have rivaled Outtz's production on occasion. But I had done my homework, determined that Outtz was the best player available, and received on-the-ground confirmation that he was healthy once again. Before making a rash decision like benching or dropping him for a potentially inferior player, I simply placed a call to the right person.

If you never ask, they will never answer. Reach out to anyone who might have more hard-nosed evidence than you and incorporate that information into your roster and lineup development. For Jo-Jo this concept is either too difficult to grasp or too hard/intimidating to implement. For you, it should be a no-brainer. Regarding your "questionable" QB, this approach means calling the team, calling/e-mailing on-the-ground reporters covering the game, and raising holy hell if necessary to get an answer. While the NFL is a much harder nut to crack than a mid-major college basketball program, all nuts are crackable. Yes, you can be that nut-cracker if you really, really want to be. You cannot go that extra mile by taking shortcuts. Do what it takes. And take what you have earned. It is not hard. It just takes time and balls.

Your pregame routine also should incorporate the impact of depth chart movements. You might learn at 11:00 a.m. that after starting the season 1-6, a team has decided to give its backup RB the starting job. Maybe this was discussed as a possibility earlier in the week. Perhaps no one seized on the news because the backup RB is untested, while the usually reliable incumbent starter is locked in a long-term contract, so the team probably will not abandon him entirely. Such news hits the wires every week, multiple times per week. Incorporating this update into your previous research, you are well positioned to make the call: Will this newly promoted RB permanently replace the former starter? And will he provide more short- and long-term value than one of your current players? If you have explored all key factors influencing his success/failure, you will know enough to make a wise decision.

In addition, you should already understand how each of your players and targeted free agents will be used in today's game, applying your superior research skills to understand each coaching staff's win strategy, and what that strategy will mean for each roster player and targeted talent. This might entail expanding the role of a little-used #3 WR to exploit an anticipated defensive matchup. Or one might anticipate a blowout between a 5-1 squad and a visiting 0-6 team, meaning the good squad's #2 RB might be in line for 10-15 carries, while the bad team's #1 RB might be rested if the game gets out of hand midway through the third quarter. Some conclusions are drawn intuitively; others stem from news sources rarely explored by fellow fantasy managers.

Remember, do what opponents are not willing or able to do. Develop casual friendships with on-the-field reporters, NFL team reps, and anyone else who might impart knowledge you cannot learn anywhere else. When searching for my first full-time job after college, I mailed 50 résumés and cover letters, earned two face-to-face interviews, and received one offer. After cultivating two-way communications between yourself and 50 NFL insiders, even if you have received only one positive response, you have gained an advantage over everyone in your league.

Fog, snow, ice, rain, and heavy winds influence fantasy production at various positions. While this is largely common sense, it bears spelling out. Some fields drain rain water better than others. Heavy, continuous snow accumulation probably will affect game conditions more than occasional flurries. If this week your starting K will kick northward and southward (based on the stadium's positioning) in a game expected to feature 40 mile-per-hour westerly winds, consider the best available one-week replacement who will kick in favorable weather. You can take an extra step by analyzing how your players have performed previously in similar weather conditions. Some QBs fare worse in frigid temperatures. Some RBs fumble more frequently in slick conditions. We all know that weather can impact player performance. The question is what you are willing to learn not merely on the macro level (general trends), but also on the micro level (individual player trends), making your research more meaningful and predictions more justifiable.

Some fantasy duds obsess over their competitors' teams. Before each week's games, these pathetic individuals examine upcoming matchups, player by player, position by position. "Cool, my QB is projected to score three more points than his QB! But oh no! My #1 RB is projected to score eight fewer points than his #1 RB! I'm gonna lose!! And no one loves me."

Jo-Jo Mc'scuses looks visibly shaken while examining a better team's roster. Hedging his bets, he rearranges his lineup to match up better against the opposition. For example, if his opponent is starting the Vikings' QB, Jo-Jo will replace his starting #3 WR (who, say, plays for the Panthers) with a different #3 WR (who happens to play for the Vikings), regardless of each WR's fantasy potential that week. "This way," Jo-Jo reasons, "I'll neutralize the impact of his QB every time he throws to my WR."

If you think this way, you have already lost. Improving your team is analogous to improving yourself: Don't do it because of someone else; do it because you are committed to personal growth. Don't make fantasy tweaks to compensate for perceived team weaknesses relative to other teams; make changes based on empirical evidence that such changes will improve your team's performance. Who cares that your opponent seems unbeatable? There is no such thing in fantasy sports anyway. You should always strive for roster perfection regardless of outside factors; otherwise you are lazy and dumb.

Earlier I discussed using karmic powers to your advantage, as well as writing letters and e-mails begging your players to shine statistically, so that, for example, dear old Grandpa can win his fantasy league and save his 80-year-old farmhouse from certain foreclosure. But the most practical approach to fantasy success starts with you and your team. What are you doing today, at this hour, at this moment to help rake in more fantasy points next week and in the weeks that follow? If your players perform as expected—based on concrete conclusions from exhaustive investigation—then you will win most regular season games and sweep through the playoffs. An empty promise? Not at all. It is about knowing more than anyone, interpreting reality better than anyone, and implementing findings faster than anyone. If you are a *kick-ass* fantasy competitor, then your claim to the title never should be questioned, especially by you.

When setting your lineup, never factor in players' past performances against teams, especially concerning games beyond a season ago. While watching a popular sports program recently, a commentator warned viewers not to start a certain WR because "he's never reached 100 yards receiving against [this week's opponent]." In dispensing this advice, this commentator failed to consider the following: In each previous game against his upcoming opponent . . .

- Was this WR covered by the same cornerback and tracked by the same safeties, all of whom are just as talented now as they were then?
- Was the same QB throwing to this WR?
- Did this WR possess the same value to his team that he has today?
- Was this WR no faster or slower than he is today?
- Was the opposing team's defensive scheme exactly the same?

And so on.

So-called "experts" make idiotic claims so often that I sometimes question why I watch. But then I remember it is also a blessing to us Dirks, as our opponents frequently listen to such meaningless recommendations, thus crippling their fantasy hopes. You see, fantasy success is not difficult to achieve. All it takes is dedication and smarts. Narrow-minded prognosticators cut corners and earn paychecks by imparting ridiculous predictions based on irrelevant statistics, when really it is nothing more than white noise. And worse than white noise, listening to it will hurt your team more often than help it.

Some analysts are better at assessing player projections on a more granular level, weighing factors that most of their colleagues simply cannot conceptualize or are too apathetic to research. These criteria include one of my favorites: motivation. I am not merely referring to an athlete *wanting it* more than someone else, though that is relevant. I am also speaking of players and coaching staffs who adjust their strategy to prevent back-to-back poor performances. I will cover this more fully in Chapter 19. But for now, understand that some of what you hear on TV or the radio, or read online or in newspapers magazines, is neither truth nor sage advice. The more you hone your *kick-ass* fantasy football sensibilities, the better you will become at distinguishing between actionable substance and plain crap.

We have explored this distinction a few times thus far with respect to online player projections; setting your roster and lineup to these untested prognostications does not make you a genius. Many weekly fantasy rankings are no better than educated guesses, and the amount of education that goes into each one varies radically. When you get burned by faulty advice, don't get mad; get the facts. Although more time-consuming, acquiring real knowledge increases your chances of winning. Based on work initiated before the draft, by Week 2 you should begin recognizing which sites yield more accurate results than others, because when it comes to making roster moves and setting your weekly lineup, you must not fall victim to that which destroys so many would-be champions. But just in case you still don't believe me, here is more *kick-ass* evidence:

In addition to tracking preseason fantasy predictions from ESPN (2009 and 2010 seasons) and CBSSports (2010 and 2011 seasons), I also have invested hundreds of hours tracking and analyzing their weekly projections and results during these same seasons. Heading into each week's games, these sites rank-ordered each player in six core positions (QB, RB, WR, TE, K, and DST), predicting which player would score the most fantasy points at each position, the second most points, the third most points, and so on. As always, the scoring system each website used for its predictions was identical to the scoring system I used to quantify each player's weekly fantasy points.

League participants the world over rely on weekly rankings to determine which players to add and drop, and also which guys to activate and reserve before each set of games. The question you would like answered (whether you realize it or not) is: Among ESPN's and CBSSports' weekly top five *prediction* rankings for each position, what was the *actual* average weekly performance ranking for these players at their respective position?

Weekly Top 5 Picks:
Average Weekly Positional Fantasy Scoring Ranking

	#1	#2	#3	#4	#5
ESPN 2009	14.41	17.69	15.76	18.40	15.76
ESPN 2010	16.63	13.75	18.38	18.99	17.01
CBSSports 2010	15.82	16.33	16.07	15.67	15.32
CBSSports 2011	12.38	12.84	13.40	15.18	17.89
Average Weekly Ranking	14.81	15.15	15.90	17.06	16.50

Just because a popular website *predicts* that QB A will be the #1 fantasy scoring QB this week does not mean QB A actually will *be* the #1 scoring QB this week. And as I have learned over the years, most websites do not even come close. In this example, ESPN's and CBSSports' weekly #1 prediction for each position actually averaged between the

14th and 15th most points at their position each week. Their #2-through-#5 predictions were, not surprisingly, even further off the mark.

Contemplate this for a moment. How often have online rankings influenced your fantasy decisions? Don't lie and say "Never" to avoid embarrassment. Confront your past and change your future, because this is no way to lead an honorable fantasy life. I value ESPN and CBSSports highly for what they do well, including reporting on late-breaking news and sharing high-level analysis from on-the-ground reporters who know what the hell they are talking about. But never allow outside rankings to shape your views unless you have verified (in my case, through hundreds of hours of research) that such rankings are consistently bankable.

Rather than limit myself merely to five picks per position per week, I also tracked both sites' weekly sixth-through-10th ranked picks, tabulating the *actual* average weekly performance ranking for these players at their respective position:

<u>Weekly Top 6-10 Picks:</u>
<u>Average Weekly Positional Fantasy Scoring Ranking</u>

	#6	#7	#8	#9	#10
ESPN 2009	18.48	17.06	18.04	18.85	16.49
ESPN 2010	15.29	16.98	17.62	17.64	18.22
CBSSports 2010	17.50	19.11	17.34	18.28	18.39
CBSSports 2011	15.91	17.37	18.12	16.95	20.68
Average Weekly Ranking	**16.80**	**17.63**	**17.78**	**17.93**	**18.44**

In addition to further substantiating my claim that not all websites produce helpful weekly rankings, these results also paint an interesting picture that, paradoxically, reflects rather positively on ESPN and CBSSports. Both sites' weekly #1 picks—however flawed—averaged the highest weekly performance ranking among all top 10 picks. Meanwhile, weekly #2 picks averaged the second highest performance ranking, and on down the line, maintaining a relatively constant regression across all 10 picks—the only modest outlier being weekly #4 picks:

Weekly Top 10 Picks: Average Weekly Positional Fantasy Scoring Ranking (by Pick)

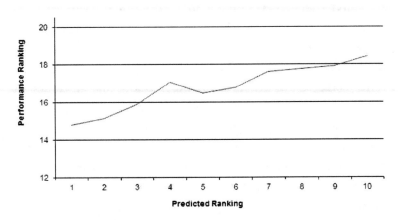

To those who stubbornly and recklessly believe these results are random and meaningless, think again. They are based on four seasons (two of which overlap), 17 weeks per season, and 10 ranking spots for six different positions per week. That amounts to more than 4,000 distinct data points that, when grouped by season, happen to produce an eerily consistent average weekly performance ranking:

Weekly Top 10 Picks: Average Weekly Positional Fantasy Scoring Ranking (by Site/Season)

	Average Performance Ranking
ESPN 2009	17.10
ESPN 2010	17.05
CBSSports 2010	16.98
CBSSports 2011	16.07

In other words, among all 1,020 of ESPN's weekly top 10 player ranking predictions, the average *actual* performance ranking for each player (naturally using the same fantasy scoring system used for each prediction) was 17.10. The following year, the average was 17.05. *Incredible.* In fact, the standard deviation for all four sets of averages is a relatively tiny 0.4236. One would expect far greater variability when accounting for the randomness/unpredictability inherent in fantasy sports.

The numbers get even stranger when separating weeks in which not all NFL teams compete (bye weeks) from weeks in which *all* NFL teams compete (non-bye weeks). For several weeks each season, two or more teams take the week off, thereby ensuring that each team plays exactly 16 games over a 17-week regular season. So how is the accuracy of ESPN's and CBSSports' projections impacted during bye week contests only?

Bye Week Top 10 Picks:
Average Weekly Positional Fantasy Scoring Ranking

	Average Bye Performance Ranking
ESPN 2009	16.88
ESPN 2010	16.05
CBSSports 2010	15.92
CBSSports 2011	14.22

With fewer teams playing during bye weeks, there are fewer players to rank. Therefore, prognosticators are likely to predict performance more accurately during these weeks (which they did in these examples, by an average of more than 1.6 rank positions versus non-bye weeks). In addition, there is greater variance in bye week predictions given the irregular number of teams (e.g. 26, 28, and 30) playing during these weeks, leading to a different set of players to rank each week; this fact is demonstrated by the relatively high .9664 standard deviation of the four analyzed sets of bye weeks.

If we sincerely wish to compare apples to apples, season by season, then we must compare players' performances from ESPN's and CBSSports' weekly top 10 rankings *when all teams compete during the same week.* By analyzing only non-bye weeks, we observe how each site fares when picking from (barring injuries and other surprises) the exact same, robust pool of players:

Non-Bye Week Top 10 Picks:
Average Weekly Positional Fantasy Scoring Ranking

	Average Non-Bye Performance Ranking
ESPN 2009	17.24
ESPN 2010	17.75
CBSSports 2010	17.73
CBSSports 2011	17.08

Simply stunning. During non-bye weeks in 2010, among the 1,200 combined top 10 ranking predictions by ESPN and CBSSports, the average *actual* player performance ranking for each site was **almost exactly the same**. In fact, the standard deviation for all four sets of averages is a miniscule *0.2956*, which is less than one-third of the variability of bye week predictions.

In light of the extraordinary uniformity of non-bye week predictions, one burning question remains: Why are ESPN and CBSSports merely mediocre at predicting which players will be each week's top 10 fantasy scorers at their position . . . and yet so *consistently* mediocre across full seasons? My hunch is that many sophisticated websites have adopted rather scientific approaches for predicting player performance. And if indeed they always employ these same methods for assigning positional rankings, then we can deduce that these methods are at least somewhat flawed.

Perhaps these formulas give too much weight to perceived advantages borne from "fantasy football conventional wisdom" without factoring the merits of such assumptions. For example, some sites might rank players slightly higher (closer to #1) when they play at home or after long layoffs (i.e. seven or more days off between games). Inversely, these sites might rank players slightly *lower* when they play on the road or after short layoffs (i.e. less than six days off between games). As you will see later, clinging to faulty logic can wreak havoc on your fantasy team, as it skews one's predictive abilities.

Of course, I don't claim to know how ESPN, CBSSports, and other deservedly reputable sites compose their less-than-helpful weekly and preseason player rankings. All we know is that, based on the comprehensive study of two seasons for each site, these rankings yielded remarkably uniform results over the seasons studied, while also producing an uncannily consistent performance ranking progression in which #1 ranked player predictions produced the highest performance ranking average, #2 players produced the second highest, and so on with only one small outlier.

This discovery should empower you as a student of Dirk. It is indeed possible to be consistently mediocre at predicting player performance across time (week by week) and across level of fantasy production (#1 rankings performing better than #2 rankings, and so on). So if consistent mediocrity exists in the fantasy universe, then why not consistent excellence?

Let's start with what we know. Suppose you are taking batting practice in a batting cage. You prearrange to swing in line with the middle of your chest on each pitch, regardless of where the ball comes. After 1,000 pitches you have made contact with the ball, say, 30% of the time, and whiffed the other half of the time. When making contact, 50% of the time you hit the ball in the sweet spot, while the other half of the time you either weakly put the ball in play or foul it off. Remember, you have swung in the exact same place on each pitch. As a result, you have surrendered control of the situation, forsaken any semblance of strategy, and simply relied on a machine to feed you perfectly placed home run balls. And you have made great contact only 15% of the time.

Jo-Jo uses a similar approach when finalizing his weekly roster and starting lineup. He trusts others—regardless of who or what they are, provided they seem like fantasy specialists—to help lead him to victory. He therefore embraces mediocrity. Taking inferior advice is like swinging in the same place again and again without considering other options. Surrendering your fantasy fate to a website's questionable predictive abilities is like leaving your batting fate to a machine that cares not one iota for your wellbeing. Only by becoming an active participant in your own fantasy fortune can you achieve such fortune.

Let's return to the batting cage. You stop automatically swinging at mid-chest level, instead opting for hundreds of hours of free-form practice. The balls continue coming at you at varied speeds and locations. But by adopting this new approach, your timing improves after a few thousand balls. You learn how and when to move to cover more of the plate. While at first repeatedly fooled by ball spin, you now pick up the ball's rotation soon after it shoots from the machine, giving you ample milliseconds to adjust your swing's speed and trajectory. Eventually you even discover vague yet exploitable patterns. While speed, spin, and location are seemingly random, after enough careful study you occasionally can predict what will *not* happen next. For example, after tens of thousands of pitches, the ball has never crossed the plate at the same height more than five times in a row. Similarly, you have not observed the same pitch type (curveball or fastball or slider, etc.) more than three times in a row.

You now have progressed beyond the *mediocre* method of entrusting your hitting prowess to a machine—of managing rosters and lineups based on others' untrained insights. Websites have little incentive to work as hard as Dirk. ESPN, CBSSports, and thousands of other sites do not compete for titles. They provide a service: fantasy reporting and advice at little-to-no cost to fantasy consumers. Some sites' reporting (i.e. ESPN's and CBSSports') is better than others' reporting. Some sites' rankings are better than others' rankings. But unless you are content being a mediocre fantasy performer, never settle for mediocre reporting or mediocre advice.

Again, no one can manage your roster and set your active lineup better than you. Your player matrix—updated continually during the week, every week—contains the most accurate player projections money can buy. Your analysis, assembled from the most timely and useful information across a wide swath of the fantasy universe, offers the strongest guidance for future player performance. And as we will continue to see, you can benefit from tiny fantasy patterns—just like the ones you spotted in the batting cage— that when combined with other tiny patterns, can transform consistent mediocrity into consistent excellence.

CHAPTER 15

WATCHING GAMES THE *KICK-ASS* WAY

"When I got my first television set,
I stopped caring so much about having close relationships."
– Andy Warhol

What I proclaimed earlier about watching preseason games relates even more to watching regular season contests. Every competition is filled with fantasological relevance not only for your current roster, but also for your future roster. Watch, interpret, research, analyze, and act on anything that will improve your title chances. I know, because I have culled an extraordinary amount of beneficial information simply by remaining attentive during games. I have watched QBs pad stats with end-of-half 50-yard bombs against prevent defenses that end harmlessly at the 20 yard line; RBs consistently falling forward when tackled, picking up one to two extra yards each time; DSTs, despite not recording a sack or turnover, succeeding in knocking down the QB nearly a dozen times and forcing him to make several errant throws.

If you are a passive manager with better things to do, then don't expect to benefit from these relatively nuanced developments, which won't show up in the box score, and which your league's online news string probably won't mention. While you read later that a QB threw for 300 yards and a TD, I actually *watched* a QB whose team trailed 31-0 at halftime, and who would have fared considerably worse if the opposing defense had not yielded so much space in the middle of the field throughout the fourth quarter. While you discover that an RB ran for 71 yards on 15 carries with no TDs, I actually *watched* an RB who did the little things to win, and whose running style is well suited for goal-line carries.

While you read that your DST netted only six fantasy points, I actually *watched* a DST capable of scoring much more.

So as you eagerly make this QB your #1 waiver pick, I invest my top selection in someone more likely to thrive in future weeks. While you shun the possibility of picking up the 15-carry RB splitting time with a teammate, I have a leg up by understanding how his performance might translate into many more fantasy points—and a larger chunk of the time-share—down the road. And when I offer a trade for your DST a few days after the game, who is better positioned to know the DST's true value and exploit his competitor's ignorance?

That is why we watch. That is why we win.

Refusing to watch football means missing every subtlety of the game, from your players' energy level to their temperament to their interaction with coaches and teammates. After catching a 32-yard TD pass on the opening drive, your #3 WR drops three passes in the second quarter and twice runs the wrong pattern (according to a TV analyst). His QB does not throw another pass to him all game. But you skipped Sunday's action to go skiing and cook s'mores with your in-laws. Even the most reliable news sites are no lock to report on the repercussions of your #3 WR's flop.

After returning from the bunny slope, you check the stats and are content to see that the WR ended the game with nine fantasy points, which generally is acceptable for tertiary receivers. But you have missed the story beyond the stats: Your #3 WR's production came on one play, after which he screwed up several times and then was ignored for the rest of the game. A couple of infrequently used receivers rose to the occasion, combining for 125 receiving yards and a score. Your #3 WR might be losing value, potentially rendering him unstartable going forward. Your Dirk-like opponents know this and can capitalize on it before you find out later this week. Your ignorance places you at a distinct disadvantage with respect to free agent pickups and trade offers.

Watching games grants insight into potential breakout candidates like untested rookies and overlooked veterans, and also augments your understanding of position battles. Suppose RB A and RB B are splitting backfield duties in Week 1, limiting each to 12-15 carries per game. Who is more explosive off the line? Who uses his blockers more effectively? Who has better breakaway speed? What you observe now could reveal which player more likely will earn 20-25 carries later, thus empowering you to invest in that potential star before anyone else does.

Sometimes in-game events are misleading, such as when a team's defense stifles RB A in the first quarter, while in the fourth quarter RB B goes off against this same defense—minus both starting linebackers, who got hurt late in the third. Rewinding to the preseason, RB A might have looked terrific playing behind his team's starting OL, while RB B looked weak running behind the team's OL rookies and soon-to-be-cut veterans. It is lazy merely to *watch* games; you must seek to *understand* what is happening and to analyze all fantasy implications. Useful Web resources often help, but are not a suitable replacement for personal observation. By investing dozens of hours each week watching players perform, you will develop more reality-based, actionable conclusions.

Some of my friends enjoy watching Sunday games at sports bars—a huge mistake for serious fantasy competitors. There are too many distractions, most screens are too small, and no DVR means no manual replays or pausing the game when your girlfriend calls looking for you. In most sports bars you cannot hear TV commentators or analysts. Although this might seem fine with you, many men and women covering games actually do a fantastic job divulging player insights, relaying injury updates, and so on. With regard to family, they might be driving you nuts, but at least you can lock the door at home and turn up the volume (good luck locking a bar and keeping them out during business hours). And unless you live in a sports bar, why would you waste valuable time commuting anywhere on game days? Twenty minutes in your car is 20 minutes not spent researching or soaking in the action.

Keep your laptop open and your favorite fantasy websites updated throughout the day. Watch as many games as you can, as intently as possible. Even if your players are locked, your aggressive fantasy mind is unlocked and loaded. As you will learn later, every injury is an opportunity (Chapter 18), while every surprisingly good or bad performance could affect one's output the following game (Chapter 19). Like the draft, game days test what you know and how you learn it. By being deeply attentive to the football world, you will be more receptive to even the most remotely useful reports, processing them, and acting on them.

Based on player performances throughout the day, record in your trusty matrix which players are more likely to outperform and underperform your earlier projections. This running tally changes throughout each week and during each game based on coaches' decisions, player motivation/interest, player injuries, injuries to other guys that affect player production, and so on. Countless factors influence one's fantasy output. Spending game days tracking these factors and assigning new expectations to hundreds of players will help you target free agents that no one else is tracking, trade for someone's undervalued players, and as you will learn in Chapter 17, drop overrated guys who are not merely replaceable, but upgradeable.

Other league owners either missed today's action or watched solely with an interest in their own roster and their opponents' lineup. You, on the other hand, are the only manager who sees the big picture. Game days are occasions to anticipate, scrutinize, and recalibrate: We anticipate player performance based on earlier research and analysis, scrutinize player performance by watching games, and recalibrate our forecasts of future player performance.

Let's return to the mail bag for another question:

Dear Sir/Madam,

My long-time wife and I worked out a deal two years ago. I get to watch the first half of every football game, and during the second half she gets to watch TLC. It's killing my fantasy team, but now I get nookie once a week.

No question here. I just wanted to tell someone that I'm still sexually active.

Sincerely,

Ralph P.
Minneapolis, Minnesota

Ralph, thanks for your letter. While it would be entirely appropriate to call you a Jo-Jo and launch into a new topic, you do bring up an interesting question for our more sexually active readers: *On game days, when is the right time for love-making?* The answer: during your 6:00 a.m. EST shower, as you (a) look and smell good enough for your wife to begrudgingly show a modicum of affection and, more importantly, (b) are not likely to miss breaking football news. Despite what some of you think, it is too late by the day's first halftime, as your ass sweat has spread to your back and legs, and your temperament has shifted from serenely confident to high-blood-pressure manic. Your wife deserves better.

Continuing with this "when is the right time" theme, some folks don't know when to use the toilet. While you can try coping for 10 hours without urinary relief, there are more admirable badges of honor to be won. The simplest solution is to wait for a game break, grab your laptop or mobile Web device, and sprint to the nearest lavatory. Depending on how well you 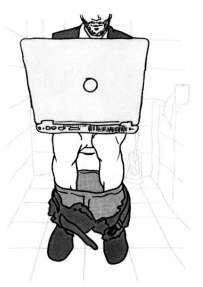 know yourself and your bathroom, you need never avert your eyes from your portable screen's play-by-play action.

When it comes to eating and drinking, steer clear of alcohol and anything else that might impair your senses. Got a cold? Avoid medicine that makes you drowsy. Anxious to gorge on a Thanksgiving feast? Avoid eating too much turkey (sleep-inducing tryptophan) and listening too much to Aunt Mae (sleep-inducing stories about yarn festivals). Also find a helper like your child or neighbor to bring food and beverages on command. If you live in the wilderness and/or lack friends or family, prepare several easy meals beforehand and keep them within easy reach of your game day resting place.

Finally, although most of us enjoy the company of pets, caretaking has its price. There are a million better things to do on game day than extricate your horny dog from a well-angled vase. Let Ginger Snap nurture her self-esteem elsewhere.

CHAPTER 16

TO TAKE OR NOT TO TAKE:
THAT IS THE FANTASY QUESTION

"He who is not courageous enough to take risks
will accomplish nothing in life."
– Muhammad Ali

Choices frequently paralyze Jo-Jo: "Should I use or save my high waiver pick?" "Should I add RB handcuffs in case my starters go down?" "With my DST playing after only three days off, should I add and start a better rested one-week replacement?" Sometimes it is wiser to *take*, and other times it is wiser *not to take*—to maintain the status quo. Your final decision should derive neither from laziness nor confusion nor ignorance; rather, it must come from the application of accumulated knowledge. Dirk knows if and when to grab a particular player throughout each week based on the athlete's prospects for short- and long-term fantasy success. Dirk's research- and analysis-driven player matrix is the basis for all decisions. As his fantasy acumen expands, his decision-making approach is refined. His assessments become more grounded . . . his team's weekly results, more accurate.

"Why would I waste my high waiver pick this week," a friend once told me, "when I can conserve it for an All-Pro-caliber player down the road?"

To the eight of you learning fantasy football from scratch, some leagues use a simple add/drop system whereby any team can pick up or discard players at any time, provided their roster and active lineup contain the required number and type of players. Other leagues restrict free agent acquisitions starting one hour (or five minutes, or some other predetermined time) before the week's opening kickoff until

Tuesday or Wednesday morning—or sometimes just during games.

Still other leagues utilize a waiver ranking system somewhat akin to the NFL, in which the team with the first waiver pick has dibs on a recently dropped player. Then the team with the second waiver pick has next dibs on a recently dropped player, followed by the team with the third waiver pick, and so on until all of that day's claims have been processed or denied. If two teams attempt to claim the same player, the team with the better waiver ranking wins the player. Any team that claims a player through this process then falls to the back of the waiver line (e.g. 12th out of 12 teams), while each of the other owners move up one spot for the next waiver opportunity. Some leagues adopt this waiver system for all roster additions, while others apply it to the initial barrage of pickups after Monday's game, and the rest of the week follows a "free for all" format of owners adding and subtracting players at will. In some leagues each team begins the season with the same amount of "fantasy dollars" with which to acquire players on an as-needed or scheduled basis.

So when it comes to adding and dropping players, there are many popular league approaches, as well as several dozen popular variations within each structure. Dirk prefers systems that reflect his lifestyle, particularly with respect to obligatory travel (see Chapter 23). However, as long as the rules are clear and fair, Dirk knows how to win simply by understanding the rules better, working harder, and being smarter than the opposition.

Now let's return to the friend I mentioned above. His 12-team league uses a waiver/free agent combo system in which recently dropped players "freeze" for two days before becoming available through waivers, while all other free agents are available on a first-come, first-served basis. By forgoing his waiver selection opportunities right after Week 1 of the 2010 season, he immediately ascended to the top of the waiver order; in other words, whenever a decent player was dropped (due to slump or demotion or some other seemingly appropriate reason), my friend had first dibs.

But week after week, this friend passed on every waiver opportunity presented to him. Most of these dropped players represented immediate roster upgrades—certainly not All-Pro caliber, but surely possessing enough talent to boost his weekly scoring by a few points. Instead of taking the gains, dropping to the back of the waiver line, and then regaining one of the top spots two to three weeks later, he kept waiting for a magic bullet. Meanwhile, his opponents continued to use their waiver picks to upgrade their teams and augment their weekly scoring potential.

The "save the high waiver pick" strategy works only when you actually *use* the pick. Don't hold your top pick for five weeks thinking you are brilliant. You are a moron for passing up countless pickups upon which your opponents are capitalizing every week. And who are you waiting for with that special selection? Some stud RB accidentally dropped by another manager? While I admire my friend's gambling spirit, fantasy stars rarely fall into one's lap. And if a stupid or shortsighted owner happens to drop one, it likely will be overturned by the commissioner or a majority of owners (depending on league rules).

But that does not mean a seemingly mediocre waiver pickup will not become a fantasy stud. Think of the handful of players each year who underperform until early-to-midseason, when suddenly they catch fire. Yet heading into Week 12, my friend was still saving his top waiver selection, while many players he bypassed eventually became regular fantasy contributors, and a few became major fantasy assets.

Rejecting roster upgrades in order to continue hoarding a high waiver pick marks one of the many perils of inaction. There are also numerous dangers to forced action. Dirk's rational approach to fantasy sports means that before choosing what course to pursue (if any), he must incorporate all known factors impacting the probability of each player's positive and negative fantasy outcomes. Meanwhile, Jo-Jo fails to anticipate soon-to-be-augmented fantasy value before it is visible to the masses. This skill entails knowing when *to take* ("This undervalued time-sharing RB is a strong candidate for 25 carries by midseason") and when *not to take* ("No current free agent would improve my roster on a weekly or season-long basis."). Attaining this skill requires unyieldingly comprehensive scrutiny.

We have already learned much from the statistical analysis outlined in this book. For example, in recent *Huddles* we observed that ESPN and CBSSports historically have underperformed when attempting to predict each week's top WR talent. Since WRs are more prevalent than other positional players, there is a tendency for more widely distributed fantasy scoring at this position. We might then conclude that it is harder to predict WRs' season-long or weekly fantasy production than it is to anticipate other positional players' fantasy production.

But does this mean WRs are more risky investments? Should we "play it safe" and insert a "more reliable" RB into our flex lineup slot? Not at all. Over the years I have earned astonishing success drafting and acquiring WRs who have produced at elite levels. They offer savvy managers many clues regarding impending fantasy production. But the central point is that you must recognize your resources and limitations. If you lack knowledge about WRs, then don't force a potentially unwise decision. If your go-to news resources consistently make accurate QB and TE predictions, then profit from this *kick-ass* information. Recognizing what you know and don't know is an elemental step in discerning whether or not to act—*to take or not to take* a certain player off waivers/free agency. Recognizing *how much* you know is a more advanced step. Making decisions based on a quantifiably reasonable probability of weekly or long-term fantasy success—that is the *kick-ass* step.

To take or not to take: that is the fantasy question based on what you know, its predictive qualities, and how confident you are that action (rather than inaction) will improve your league title chances. Dirk repeats this process thousands of times throughout each fantasy season. When probability of success exceeds a certain percentage—it is different for each person depending on his comfort level with risk taking—then he acts swiftly, leaving no time for opponents to usurp his claim. When probability of success does not cross this threshold, then he refrains from action no matter what his instincts, horoscope, or father-in-law tell him. This is why Dirk-like diligence is the only way to win your league consistently; if your research is half-assed, then your probability assessment, and thus your basis for *taking* or *not taking*, is meaningless. Only by collecting superior information from superior resources can you proceed with superior confidence.

One dilemma often facing fantasy managers is whether to bolster their roster reserves with positional handcuffs, particularly after the season's midpoint. In case you are not familiar with this technique, here is an example: You have two elite-level RBs filling a maximum of two RB lineup spots. Each team's bye has passed, meaning that barring an injury or some other hindrance, these two players likely will continue generating terrific fantasy point totals. Each RB's backup is essentially worthless, averaging no more than five touches per game. Of your four reserve players, two are decent RBs with 10-12 carries per game. Their future value hinges on various factors such as whether they earn more touches, whether they become more versatile offensive threats (e.g. more receiving opportunities), whether each coaching staff focuses more on the running game, etc.

So your question is, "Should I drop one or both reserve RBs in order to add one or both RB backups?" When confronting this *take or not to take* quandary, a common mistake is assuming that one has nothing to lose by grabbing the backup RBs. After all, each of your current reserve RBs average only seven fantasy points per game. If forced into starting roles, the backup RBs should post much better numbers. Another mistake is assuming that these backups are worthless, or that it is dumb to position your team for a minor roster catastrophe, as you always can find a replacement if or when one of your premier RBs gets hurt.

Neither decision is justifiable when viewed in a vacuum. We must examine options more carefully, beginning by answering the following questions:

- Has either backup RB ever assumed a lead-back role, and if so, how did he perform?
    - During these performances, how closely did that team's coaching style, OL, and other factors align with those of his current team?
- What is the likelihood that a backup RB, if forced into action due to a premier RB's injury, will split carries with his team's third-string RB?
- Based on the quantity and severity of their past injuries, what is the likelihood that either starting RB will get hurt and miss time?
- Has either reserve RB assumed a lead-back role, and if so, how did he perform?
    - During these performances, how closely did that team's coaching style, OL, and other factors align with those of his current team?
- Does either reserve RB provide more short- and long-term value (potential fantasy points) than any available free agent—RB or otherwise?

- Is either reserve RB more likely to start later this season than either backup RB you are targeting?

I could go on, but you get the point. Too many Jo-Jos adopt one-size-fits-all strategies without honoring each situation's uniqueness. I have met people who consistently stockpile handcuffs as the playoffs draw near, stubbornly clinging to the narrow notion that all such backups will thrive if elevated to starter. And I have met others who consider this tactic a waste of resources, opting instead to collect the best talent currently available without weighing the impact of a potentially devastating injury.

Each approach presents unnecessary risks based on ignorance. Strategies must be based on sound science, not baseless traditions. The more accurate your decisions, the more points your team will score, and the more likely you will be crowned champion.

Sometimes such science goes beyond statistics, injury risk, and coaching schemes. Sometimes our decision to *take* a player comes, in part, from what we know about that player's personality in light of various circumstances. In the following changing scenarios, figure out whether each player is most likely to thrive, sustain past numbers, or wilt. Think of this as a new GRE section to test whether students are better suited for a fantasy sports degree:

- A rookie #1 QB is called out by his head coach for making poor on-field decisions.
- A 2-9 team's #1 RB publicly questions his teammates' intensity after another blowout loss.
- A team's #1 WR is traded midseason, becoming the #2 WR on his new team.
- A predominantly pass-blocking #1 TE tells a reporter that he wants to catch more passes.

- A #1 K takes the blame for missing three field goals after a tough loss.
- A rival team's center publicly states that an aging star linebacker on a #1 DST has "lost a step."

There are thousands of interesting circumstances we witness all the time, yet unfortunately don't have time to discuss. But the point is that you don't require a psychology degree to study the psychological effects of words and actions. When you next hear about a situation like the ones above, observe how the noted player(s) perform the following week, and then the week after that. Some athletes flourish when tested, while others crumple under the pressure. Imagine how your sizable league advantage will grow after applying such hard-nosed analysis to your *take or not to take* decisions.

While competing in the 2005 *SportingNews* Salary Cap Football Challenge, I employed a range of *kick-ass* techniques described in this book, including tapping into the psychology of players before adding them to my team. In this 200,000-person contest, each competitor could start any lineup each week, provided that each position was filled as required, and as long as his lineup's total value did not exceed his team's salary cap. Hundreds of factors influenced one's success, including finding the most promising weekly talent that few other competitors could spot. So if 150,000 people started Peyton Manning one week, and my diligent research led me to start QB ABC instead, then if QB ABC scored more fantasy points than Manning that week, advantage *me*. If Manning fared better, advantage 150,000 other people. Since I finished the contest in 19th place overall, more often than not I made better decisions than 99.99% of my opponents.

One of these decisions came six weeks into the season. During my customary *kick-ass* routine I found a news article highlighting how RB LaMont Jordan wanted more carries. In his previous game against the Chargers, he ran only 12 times—though he scored twice. His team, the Raiders, lost that game 27-14 and now were languishing with a 1-4 record. Jordan was averaging only 17.4 carries per game and seemed to deserve more based on how well he was playing with relatively limited opportunities. The Raiders needed a win to turn things around before their season got out of hand. Their next game would be a home tilt against the Bills, which had yielded an average of 158.5 rushing yards and 1.17 rushing TDs per game. It was a perfect storm for success.

Would Oakland heed its star RB's public request? Or would Jordan's appeal fall on deaf ears? Based on what I read and learned about player, team, and context, I filled one of my two *SportingNews* league RB slots with Jordan. Given the large pool of talented RBs available, most of my competitors selected more "elite" talent. Despite averaging one TD in each of his first five games, Jordan had exceeded 70 rushing yards only once and was netting a mere 3.56 yards per carry. Why risk a roster spot on a supposedly mediocre option? Well that is the difference between Jo-Jo and Dirk. Jo-Jo plays it safe. Dirk takes calculated risks with a higher probability of success than what the status quo can offer. When *taking* more likely will yield positive results than *not taking*, then act on it. And my research showed that Jordan had the highest upside of any RB that week.

The result: Oakland gave its starting RB what he wanted. In a 38-17 thumping of Buffalo, the undervalued Jordan carried a season-high 28 times for 122 yards and three TDs, also tacking on four catches for 40 yards. That translated to 32 fantasy points in my CBSSports league. For context, in 2011 only three RBs totaled more than 32 fantasy points in a game. Jordan achieved something special that day. And only a small percentage of us expected it. So factor what players say into the rest of your analysis. There is value in desire.

During draft prep we learned the power of testing fantasy football hypotheses, a process in which we ask a question with no known answer, conduct applicable research, and determine whether there is sufficient evidence to influence future fantasy behavior. Such testing requires access to quantitative data, of which there should be plenty; after all, would there be sports without statistics? But that does not ensure the availability of needed stats. Often a little digging is required.

Before writing this book I invested many hundreds of hours gathering and testing data in ways that no one else has done. While you are benefitting from the expertise I have painstakingly acquired, this does not give you license to slack off. Keep enlarging your pool of fantasy football knowledge in order to continue increasing your advantage over league competitors. The results of my research and analysis are merely a speck in the fantasy universe. Devote your life to discovering more specks.

The following are a few of the many questions I have sought to answer over the years, each of which offers clues on when to *take* and when *not to take*:

Home Field Advantage

Do the NFL's best positional players score more fantasy points at home versus on the road?

I always assumed that NFL players performed better at home than on the road. Having never placed this theory under a microscope, my reasoning was at best shallow and at worst harmful. Sure, home teams tend to win more NFL games than road teams. For example, between 2008 and

2011 (not counting the one tie game in 2008), home teams won nearly 57% of their games:

Home Team Winning Percentage

	Home Wins	Home Losses	Home Win %
2008	146	109	**57.25%**
2009	146	110	**57.03%**
2010	143	113	**55.86%**
2011	145	111	**56.64%**
		Average Home Win %	**56.72%**

Home clubs' year-by-year win rate was remarkably consistent, with a standard deviation of .5293. While no one knows how long this trend will continue, we now have empirical evidence that, by a relatively small yet distinct margin, home teams have won more often than road teams in recent years. Therefore, when two relatively equal teams compete, we can assign some probability that the home team will win. This is not rocket science or a Nobel Prize-worthy discovery. I simply am starting with a basic premise and then demonstrating how that premise can be supported.

Now we turn to the question of whether a team's home field advantage influences its players' fantasy production and, by extension, whether it should help guide my daily fantasy decision making concerning free agents, trades, and lineup shifts. For the top 20 players at each position, I tracked their fantasy point production for home games versus road games. To maintain consistency, I adopted the same fairly standard fantasy points system based on leagues in which I have competed (one point per 40 passing yards, one point per 10 rushing yards, one point per 10 receiving yards, six points per TD, minus two points per offensive turnover, two points per defensive turnover, one point per extra point, minus three points per missed extra point, etc.). To help ensure valid and reliable results, I did not include stats for each season's final two games, during which some playoff-bound teams rest their best players, while a few other teams are inclined to rest or limit star players who normally would play, but who need not risk further injury for relatively meaningless matchups.

The following table shows that between 2008 and 2010, the top 20 players per position averaged 0.95 more fantasy points per home game than per road game. RBs and QBs enjoyed the greatest home field edge, while WRs performed nearly as well on the road as at home:

Top 20 Players per Position:
Home Field Fantasy Points Advantage

	QB	RB	WR	TE	K	DST	Avg Fantasy Point Differential
2008	2.75	1.70	0.10	1.21	-0.12	1.95	**1.27**
2009	1.44	2.03	0.28	0.52	1.57	0.42	**1.04**
2010	0.23	1.89	-0.26	0.39	0.73	0.35	**0.55**
Avg Fantasy Point Differential	**1.47**	**1.87**	**0.04**	**0.71**	**0.73**	**0.90**	**0.95**

Then I narrowed my research to include only the top *10* players per position, wondering whether more elite talent would benefit even more from playing in their home stadium. However, as you can see below, their per-game home field advantage surprisingly was still 0.95 fantasy points. Moreover, RBs and QBs continued to hold the strongest home field advantage (though QBs now led the way), while WRs still performed just a hair better at home than on the road:

Top 10 Players per Position:
Home Field Fantasy Points Advantage

	QB	RB	WR	TE	K	DST	Avg Fantasy Point Differential
2008	4.67	1.67	0.88	0.67	-0.55	1.29	**1.44**
2009	1.15	1.95	0.67	-0.83	1.84	2.42	**1.20**
2010	0.20	1.77	-1.28	1.24	0.46	-1.14	**0.21**
Avg Fantasy Point Differential	2.01	1.80	0.09	0.36	0.59	0.86	0.95

"It's only a 0.95-point advantage," you insist. "Your research is pretty meaningless." Really? I expected more from you at this stage. These results appear modest when examined individually. Yet when viewed collectively, they kick ass. During the 2008-2010 fantasy seasons, suppose your active lineup consisted of one QB, two RBs, two WRs, one TE, one K, and one DST, and to simplify this scenario, assume that each one is a top 20 player at their respective position. Based on the above findings for top 20 players, your lineup would have averaged 7.64 more fantasy points per home game than per road game:

Top 20 Players per Position:
Home Field Fantasy Points Advantage (Starting Lineup)

	QB	2 RBs	2 WRs	TE	K	DST	Lineup Fantasy Point Differential
2008	2.75	3.40	0.20	1.21	-0.12	1.95	**9.39**
2009	1.44	4.06	0.56	0.52	1.57	0.42	**8.56**
2010	0.23	3.78	-0.53	0.39	0.73	0.35	**4.96**
Lineup Fantasy Point Differential	1.47	3.75	0.08	0.71	0.73	0.90	7.64

Some people are lucky enough / Dirk-like to possess a lineup filled with top 10 players. How would home games have affected their fantasy point production during the 2008, 2009, and 2010 seasons?

Top 10 Players per Position:
Home Field Fantasy Points Advantage (Starting Lineup)

	QB	2 RBs	2 WRs	TE	K	DST	Lineup Fantasy Point Differential
2008	4.67	3.34	1.76	0.67	-0.55	1.29	**11.19**
2009	1.15	3.90	1.34	-0.83	1.84	2.42	**9.82**
2010	0.20	3.54	-2.56	1.24	0.46	-1.14	**1.73**
Lineup Fantasy Point Differential	**2.01**	**3.59**	**0.18**	**0.36**	**0.59**	**0.86**	**7.58**

So even when starting top 10 players from each position, your lineup would have averaged 7.58 more fantasy points per home game than per road game—almost identical, as it turns out, to their mid-tier brethren ranked 11th to 20th at each position. The overall drop-off in 2010 was severe, though the boon to your team in 2008 and 2009 would have been tremendous.

We cannot prove that fantasy players' home field advantage will continue in the future. Was 2010 an outlier or a trendsetter? More research is needed. But remember that winning your league does not require knowledge of absolute truths. It simply requires assembling an optimal roster and configuring a lineup that maximizes the probability of winning that week while not adversely impacting long-term success.

Our sport is about *probabilities.* We formulate a hypothesis and test it; if it bears fruit, we assign a probability based on its application. With three years of data and analysis under my belt, I believe there is a high probability that between two RBs of equal fantasy ability, with all other factors (OL, opposing defense, touches per game, health, etc.) being equal, the RB playing at home will score more fantasy points than the RB playing on the road. This may seem obvious now. But before I offered empirical evidence, this idea was merely an unsubstantiated hunch. By gathering evidence related to other factors (OL, opposing defense, touches per game, health, etc.), we begin to paint a picture of fantasy dominance, where each examined hypothesis is another brush stroke on the canvas.

Whether seeking a one-week pickup or a long-term solution, when scouring the waiver wire for a roster addition, consider candidates' remaining home/away schedules. Unless proven otherwise through additional research (for example, of *all* players at each position, instead of just the top 20), I now believe there is a good probability that these players (except WRs) will score more fantasy points at home than on the road. I use this information to score a few extra points per week. You should, too.

Long Layoff Advantage

Do the NFL's best positional players average more fantasy points in games following a 7+ day layoff, as opposed to games after briefer layoffs?

Some prognosticators favor players who have extra time off between games: "[DST 1] is my #1 defensive pick this week, as the extra days off should make them well rested for this important battle." Still others warn that these same players will be rusty after longer-than-normal breaks: "Expect [QB 1] to be a little out of sync with his offense, as he has not played since before the bye." How can allegedly smart people hold diametrically opposing theories? Have you ever wondered what a statistical analysis would show?

Once again I completed a comprehensive three-year analysis of each position's top 20 players to determine whether they scored more fantasy points when playing after seven or more days off between games (e.g. playing on Monday after playing on Sunday the previous week), versus the more customary six days off between games (e.g. playing on consecutive Sundays) or less. I applied the same standard fantasy scoring as before and again excluded the last two games of each season.

Between 2008 and 2010, the top 20 players per position averaged 0.85 more fantasy points in games following 7+ day layoffs. Just as with our home field advantage findings, QBs and RBs held the largest extended layoff advantage, while TEs and DSTs owned the least advantage—and in fact, TEs' 2010 performances pushed them into negative territory over the three-year period, translating into a net disadvantage when playing after long breaks:

Top 20 Players per Position:
Long Layoff Fantasy Points Advantage

	QB	RB	WR	TE	K	DST	Avg Fantasy Point Differential
2008	0.57	3.16	1.50	0.62	0.95	0.55	**1.22**
2009	2.10	0.46	-0.59	1.12	0.56	-0.34	**0.55**
2010	2.05	0.89	2.33	-2.10	1.35	0.19	**0.79**
Avg Fantasy Point Differential	1.57	1.51	1.08	-0.12	0.95	0.14	0.85

When narrowing my research to the top *10* players per position, we observe much greater advantages across five positions. WRs were the only elite positional players to perform worse than their secondary-tier counterparts after a 7+ day break:

Top 10 Players per Position:
Long Layoff Fantasy Points Advantage

	QB	RB	WR	TE	K	DST	Avg Fantasy Point Differential
2008	2.57	2.41	-0.12	1.50	1.90	0.29	**1.43**
2009	3.94	1.36	-1.19	2.27	0.91	0.76	**1.34**
2010	2.57	3.21	0.45	-2.45	1.64	1.81	**1.20**
Avg Fantasy Point Differential	3.03	2.33	-0.28	0.44	1.48	0.95	1.32

What does this mean for your fantasy team? Let's see how a top 20 lineup consisting of one QB, two RBs, two WRs, one TE, one K, and one DST would have fared, on average, in games immediately following 7+ day breaks. In the table below we observe that a lineup filled with elite- and secondary-level players coming off a 7+ day layoff would have averaged 7.71 more fantasy points than normal per week between 2008 and 2010:

Top 20 Players per Position: Long Layoff
Fantasy Points Advantage (Starting Lineup)

	QB	2 RBs	2 WRs	TE	K	DST	Lineup Fantasy Point Differential
2008	0.57	6.33	3.00	0.62	0.95	0.55	**12.00**
2009	2.10	0.93	-1.19	1.12	0.56	-0.34	**3.18**
2010	2.05	1.79	4.66	-2.10	1.35	0.19	**7.94**
Lineup Fantasy Point Differential	1.57	3.01	2.16	-0.12	0.95	0.14	7.71

When factoring lineups comprised only of top *10* positional players, your edge would have expanded to nearly 10 points per week:

Top 10 Players per Position: Long Layoff
Fantasy Points Advantage (Starting Lineup)

	QB	2 RBs	2 WRs	TE	K	DST	Lineup Fantasy Point Differential
2008	2.57	4.83	-0.24	1.50	1.90	0.29	**10.85**
2009	3.94	2.71	-2.37	2.27	0.91	0.76	**8.21**
2010	2.57	6.41	0.90	-2.45	1.64	1.81	**10.89**
Lineup Fantasy Point Differential	3.03	4.65	-0.57	0.44	1.48	0.95	**9.98**

So how do you put these findings into practice during your fantasy season? Naturally, finding eight worthy players to start after seven or more days off is not easy. But situations arise throughout each season that demand smart choices among multiple options. Imagine you must start one of two DSTs ranked in the top 10 in fantasy points. DST A is coming off a bye and playing at home, while DST B will play on the road after the usual six days off (Sunday to Sunday). After reading this book you know that between 2008 and 2010, elite-level, home-playing DSTs have a built-in advantage over regular-layoffed, road-traveling DSTs. Therefore, you could predict with some confidence that DST A will score more fantasy points than DST B this week *solely* based on home field and layoff factors. When tallying other criteria such as health, weather conditions, opposing offense, and so on, you have more tools with which to make an even sounder prediction.

This is how we maximize the return on knowledge. No longer grabbing players in the dark, you are evolving into a *kick-ass* manager who makes deliberate decisions based on all available evidence. A three-point advantage here, a two-point edge there, and soon you will create your own statistically probable formula for predicting success—and not only from your stud performers, but also from "mediocre" players who face ideal fantasy conditions.

Short Layoff Advantage

Do the NFL's best positional players average more fantasy points in games following less than six days off, as opposed to games after 6+ day layoffs?

This question is based on the premise shared by many prognosticators that players coming off "short weeks" face a disadvantage versus those who have enjoyed regular or extended rest. For example, suppose your #1 RB just played on Monday night. His next game is this Sunday afternoon, equating to five days off between games, which anyone who has not studied this matter will tell you is a potential red flag: "After carrying a full load Monday night, [RB A] could be a bit tired heading into this key divisional matchup."

But basing your *take* and *not to take* decisions on concrete historical data is far more reliable than heeding advice from someone with no personal stake in your fantasy success. While we might not like what is learned through this approach, we cannot dismiss its implications.

My three-year analysis of each position's top 20 players tested whether they scored more fantasy points when playing six days or less after their previous game (fewer than six days off), versus the more customary schedule of six days off between games (e.g. playing on consecutive Sundays) or more. I applied the same fantasy scoring methodology as with the other two studies, and again excluded the last two games of each season. Surprisingly (to any "expert" who never researches this stuff), these supposedly exhausted players—from all six positions—actually averaged more fantasy points on short rest than during normal or extended breaks:

Top 20 Players per Position:
Short Layoff Fantasy Points Advantage

	QB	RB	WR	TE	K	DST	Avg Fantasy Point Differential
2008	4.98	0.45	2.50	1.34	1.64	2.09	**2.16**
2009	-2.32	3.99	-1.00	-2.23	1.39	1.06	**0.15**
2010	-0.41	0.46	0.67	1.88	0.80	-1.47	**0.32**
Avg Fantasy Point Differential	**0.75**	**1.64**	**0.72**	**0.33**	**1.27**	**0.56**	**0.88**

When extricating each season's top 10 players per position, four of the six positions (QB, RB, WR, and DST) exhibited even greater fantasy scoring prowess after short layoffs:

Top 10 Players per Position:
Short Layoff Fantasy Points Advantage

	QB	RB	WR	TE	K	DST	Avg Fantasy Point Differential
2008	6.28	-0.36	3.36	0.16	0.87	0.74	**1.84**
2009	-3.72	5.53	-0.02	-2.57	2.24	1.37	**0.47**
2010	2.27	0.59	1.90	2.72	-0.38	1.88	**1.50**
Avg Fantasy Point Differential	**1.61**	**1.92**	**1.75**	**0.10**	**0.91**	**1.33**	**1.27**

Next we examine how these results would have impacted your fantasy scoring output between 2008 and 2010, assuming a lineup comprising one QB, two RBs, two WRs, one TE, one K, and one DST. Drawing from each position's top 20 players, your lineup would have netted 7.63 more points per game when playing less than seven days after their previous game. Remember, some of these athletes would have been "mediocre" free agents in your league who, under the right conditions (like this one), could have helped your team:

Top 20 Players per Position: Short Layoff
Fantasy Points Advantage (Starting Lineup)

	QB	2 RBs	2 WRs	TE	K	DST	Lineup Fantasy Point Differential
2008	4.98	0.91	4.99	1.34	1.64	2.09	**15.94**
2009	-2.32	7.99	-1.99	-2.23	1.39	1.06	**3.89**
2010	-0.41	0.93	1.34	1.88	0.80	-1.47	**3.07**
Lineup Fantasy Point Differential	0.75	3.28	1.45	0.33	1.27	0.56	7.63

When examining a lineup consisting only of top 10 players, thanks to the success of RBs and WRs, your team would have averaged more than 11 extra points per game when playing on short rest versus all other game schedule scenarios:

Top 10 Players per Position: Short Layoff
Fantasy Points Advantage (Starting Lineup)

	QB	2 RBs	2 WRs	TE	K	DST	Lineup Fantasy Point Differential
2008	6.28	-0.71	6.71	0.16	0.87	0.74	**14.04**
2009	-3.72	11.06	-0.03	-2.57	2.24	1.37	**8.35**
2010	2.27	1.18	3.80	2.72	-0.38	1.88	**11.48**
Lineup Fantasy Point Differential	1.61	3.84	3.49	0.10	0.91	1.33	11.29

This is a lot to take in, so take a moment to digest it while I bombard you with more information. In particular I want to synthesize these historical nuggets of truth into one unified concept. Examine the following two tables. Then get back to me:

Top 20 Players per Position:
Long/Short Layoff Comparison

	Avg Fantasy Point Differential	Lineup Fantasy Point Differential
7+ Days Rest -- Top 20	0.85	7.71
< 6 Days Rest -- Top 20	0.88	7.63

Top 10 Players per Position:
Long/Short Layoff Comparison

	Avg Fantasy Point Differential	Lineup Fantasy Point Differential
7+ Days Rest -- Top 10	1.32	9.98
< 6 Days Rest -- Top 10	1.27	11.29

A funny thing happened between 2008 and 2010. Who knows whether this three-year period marks a statistical oddity or trend. We know only what we observe in the data, which I have collected and analyzed to determine whether it contains anything fantasologically actionable. And this is what we see:

(1) Regardless of whether top 20 players received extra rest or less-than-customary rest between games, they yielded almost the same combined per-game fantasy point advantage and team lineup fantasy point advantage.

(2) Regardless of whether top 10 players received extra or less-than-customary rest between games, they yielded almost the same per-game fantasy

point advantage, with a moderately similar team lineup fantasy point advantage.

Who would have thought that a lineup of top 10 players competing after abbreviated breaks would have given you not only 11+ extra points per game versus lineups competing after normal (Sunday-to-Sunday) breaks, but also more than one extra point per game versus lineups competing after long breaks? And who would have conceived the lack of any meaningful statistical difference among the other three modes of comparison (top 10 average, top 20 average, and top 20 lineup)? Apparently the only schedule scenario in which top 10 / top 20 players underperformed (on average) was when playing after normal breaks. Go figure.

What once would have seemed insane now must be factored into our daily thinking. I am not claiming that home field, long layoff, and short layoff scenarios are the most important factors to consider when *taking* or *not taking*. And as you know, I am not declaring that what we witnessed in 2008-2010 is part of a century-long or even decade-long pattern. I am merely affirming the statistical probability that each position's top 20 players—and often more so among top 10 players—will earn more fantasy points than otherwise when playing at home, after a long break, or after a short break. These are three more instruments among many that can help you make more rational, statistically supportable, *kick-ass* decisions.

When it comes to addressing the common dilemma, *to take or not to take*, you can choose the easy road or the much more difficult one. The easy road will lead more often to failure. The very difficult one will help you pinpoint whether and when to replace a player with another, or to start one player over another. It is one of the hardest skills to learn, and also is one of the most rewarding.

CHAPTER 17

THE RIGHT TIME TO CUT A PLAYER LOOSE

"It's not the daily increase but daily decrease. Hack away at the unessential."
– Bruce Lee

Saying good-bye to a loved one is hard sometimes. Telling my wife before each NFL season that I will be emotionally unavailable for several months is always tough on her. After bidding farewell to family and friends (except friends competing in my leagues), I am not too much of a man to acknowledge the shedding of a few tears. And yes, occasionally one of these tears is mine. We Dirks must make sacrifices for the greater good, for what good are we to others when we finish in ninth place out of 12 teams? To know fantasy football victory, we must embrace the temporary loss of a life once led. In this way we honor the memory of neglected family and friends through fantasy achievements and prize money.

But Jo-Jo extends this oversensitivity to fantasy football, and therein lies the problem. How can he make *kick-ass* decisions affecting players he considers distant friends? Dropping an athlete from his roster is akin to dumping a buddy on the side of the road and saying, "You can hitch from here."

I would need many hundreds of hands to have enough fingers to count the number of players who have graced me with their presence and sufficiently high fantasy point totals, only to be restored to free agency once other players usurped their value. Yet nary has a day passed when I felt a personal connection to any athlete even closely resembling my fondness for my childhood pet guinea pigs, let alone friends and family. Gifted athletes they are; lifelong pals they are not.

Oh! the wretchedness of Jo-Jo, who likens his players to comrades-in-arms. Lacking real-world companionship, this lonely soul aches for one-sided personal relationships with NFL players he will come to know neither intimately nor platonically. "I don't know what I'd do without Ray Rice," he whines into his asthma inhaler. He sleeps easier at night knowing that Rice is his team's cornerstone and will somehow set a good example for the rest of his players.

Oh! sad days for he who operates with his heart rather than his head. My friend Matt was such an unfortunate, although I heard he has since moderated his fantasy priorities somewhat. A diehard Bengals and Reds fan since childhood, Matt used to manage teams stacked with far too much hometown talent. Season after season he sacrificed quality—and by extension, fantasy championships—in exchange for added incentive to cheer on his beloved teams. When stuck with an overvalued and underperforming Cincinnati WR, he exhibited loyalty far exceeding even the typical Jo-Jo. He deserved warm praise for such selfless and unrequited devotion. He also deserved zero titles, which is what he earned.

To those who carve out roster spots for favorite players, often at a steep price, I ask, "Why love players who cannot love you back?" Why shave several fantasy points off your weekly scoring potential simply because you want to root for your favorite team with *110%* intensity instead of the normally adequate 100%? If you need extra fantasy incentive to support the Cowboys or Patriots, are you really that much of a fan to begin with? Or are you more concerned about someone else drafting your favorite QB, thus turning you into a weekly fantasy contortionist as you root *for* your fantasy team, *for* your favorite NFL team, and *against* the field general on whom you possess a secret man-crush?

A recent comment from my friend Mark (no, not that Mark, and not the other Mark either) was apropos to his condition/ailment: "Fantasy sports takes away from rooting for your favorite team." For this Mark, professional team loyalty trumps fantasy team loyalty. To paraphrase Jerry Seinfeld, Mark roots for laundry—in his case cheering for anyone being paid to play football in a Steelers jersey. And he is happy with that arrangement. And that is why, dear readers, the *kick-ass* fantasy lifestyle is not for everyone.

If you are like Mark, or like the former iteration of Matt, you are not of sound mind to know when to cut a player loose. You cling to guys like they are BFFs (Best Friends Forever), when they are actually BFFs (Bad Fantasy Footballers). You would not remain friends with someone who lets you down week after week. Why the double-standard?

Dirk drops players without a trace of guilt, and with the same purpose and conviction applied to all fantasy decisions. Who cares that the QB who helped you reach last year's semifinals is the same QB who contributed to your 5-1 start this season? If you are now 5-4, in part, because three weeks ago this same QB lost his #1 WR and center to season-ending injuries, and as a result has averaged 11 fantasy points in each of the past three weeks as defenses have exposed his team's personnel deficiencies, and if team management is not committed to filling the WR and center holes, and if there is a QB on waivers who possesses a greater probability of short- and long-term fantasy prowess, then WHAT IN GOD'S NAME ARE YOU WAITING FOR? You think this QB will thank you for not abandoning him in his time of greatest need?

Kick-ass fantasy owners like me constantly evaluate our rosters for weaknesses. With the advent of fresh NFL player and team information throughout each day, we remain vigilantly skeptical even of our top performers, knowing that at any time an injury, suspension, demotion, or bad case of the crazies could reduce our loaded team to fantasy ruin. While an investment in a fluctuating market is terrific when outperforming expectations, don't be left holding the money when its prospects dim.

For more insight into a dilemma confounding many of you on a weekly basis, let us turn to a parable.

The Parable of the Unfruitful Tight End

A manager inserted a tight end into his lineup and watched again and again to see if he would produce points, but he was always disappointed.

Finally he told his co-manager, "We have waited three weeks, and he has not accrued more than 25 receiving yards in any game! We have to cut him. He is just taking up space on our team."

The co-manager answered, "Give him one more chance. Leave him in the lineup another week, as he has been getting more looks in practice. If he catches some passes next week, fine. If not, then we can cut him."

Have you ever adopted a "Let's give him one more chance" approach? Maybe your fourth round pick—a #2 RB—has netted only 20 fantasy points through four games. You blindly commit to starting him one more week, postponing warranted research and a potentially sensible decision until after you can "get another look" at your underperformer in action.

This approach reflects a dedication not to excellence, but to futility. You have surrendered control of your team to guessing, hoping, and delaying. You are better than that. Your continually updated player matrix should offer strong clues on which player(s) would provide more short- and long-term value than an athlete whose best fantasy days are numbered—or in the past. Assess every known factor and assign fantasy point probabilities for each player. If your team would be better with someone else, act on it. Immediately.

One anecdote reveals the value of knowing when to cut a player, while also reminding us that some things cannot be predicted. Heading into Week 8 in 2010, I wondered whether the fantasy potential of the Chicago Bears' Jay Cutler, my incumbent QB who was readying for a bye, had fallen below that of any free agent QBs. I determined that available starters Mark Sanchez (Jets), Jon Kitna (Cowboys), and Matthew Stafford (Lions) were potential replacements. All three were facing relatively weak pass defenses in their upcoming contests. There were modest differentiators that affected all four QBs' long-term fantasy potential such as season schedule and playmaking receiver options, but nothing to provoke a roster change—that is, until I analyzed each team's propensity to pass.

When comparing all four QBs' teams through the first seven weeks, the Lions had yielded more points per game than the Jets and Bears, but not as many as the Cowboys, who were near the top of this list. As we learned in Chapter 10, teams with the *most points against* tend to average more passing attempts per game than those with the *fewest points against*. Frequently playing from behind, would the 1-5 Cowboys lean on the 38-year-old Kitna the rest of the season? Seeking more conclusive evidence, I researched each team's propensity to run and pass. This turned out to be the breakthrough: Through Week 7, approximately two-thirds of the Lions' plays were passes, whereas the other three teams were much more run-heavy. After establishing that this differentiator significantly impacted each QB's probability of future fantasy points, and after further examining Stafford's fantasy stud potential, I replaced my incumbent QB with Stafford.

At first my research paid off. Stafford threw four TDs that Sunday and finished with 29 fantasy points—#2 among QBs that week. Kitna finished in 18th place. Sanchez tied for 25th. Stafford went on to score an exceptional 24 points in Week 9 . . . before succumbing to a season-ending injury in the fourth quarter.

"Stupid move," you say. "You dropped a perfectly respectable QB [Cutler], and two weeks later you were back where you started, needing yet another QB replacement."

This is why I bring up this anecdote. I am not infallible, because fantasy football is a game of chance, and I am no psychic. We Dirks deal in probabilities, not absolutes. Through exhaustive study, I determined that Stafford offered the highest probability of the most per-game fantasy points among all free agent QBs. Until he got hurt, my supposition was correct. Moreover, Stafford proved to be not merely a run-of-the-mill free agent acquisition, but rather an elite fantasy talent.

This initial detailed study was the foundation of my July 2011 pre-draft analysis, through which (as you know) I targeted Stafford as one of fantasy football's most undervalued QBs. I knew that, if healthy, he was capable of being a top five QB. My friends thought I was crazy. Most "experts" gave him little chance. But when he finished the 2011 season ranked fourth in fantasy points *among all players*, I was not surprised.

Additionally, in this 14-team league my team scored the second most fantasy points in Week 8 and tied for the most in Week 9. If not for Stafford's heroics, I likely would have suffered a couple of devastating defeats. And in case you were wondering (and you should), Cutler averaged a pedestrian 14.1 fantasy points per game after Week 7 and wrapped up the year ranked 15th in QB fantasy points. Kitna averaged 13.9 points per game the rest of the way. Sanchez: only 10.9 points. In Week 8 I concluded that Cutler was not the best short- and long-term QB option available. That meant he was droppable. No hesitation. No hedging. Neither Kitna nor Sanchez was the best replacement. Stafford was. Once you learn and adopt this *kick-ass* approach, you will know the right time to drop a player . . . every time.

Cutting players is the natural order of things. Get that through your sentimental head. Don't expect to finish the season with the same roster you drafted. In fact, based on the law of averages, you are highly unlikely to win the championship if you maintain the same lineup throughout. Most great players experience off days every now and then. All good players perform poorly even more often. And as we learned in Chapter 3, many mediocre players are primed for a few big fantasy payoffs each season, often at the expense of the first two groups. So stop protecting your roster. Drop dead weight before it weighs down your victory prospects. Replace them with athletes who possess the highest probability of short- and long-term fantasy success.

I sat down with Jo-Jo this morning to learn more about what makes this fantasy non-icon tick:

Me: What makes you tick, Jo-Jo?

Jo-Jo: There are so many things.

Me: *Then name just one.*

Jo-Jo: *I'm kinda nervous.*

Me: *Let's try a new question. What's your strategy for deciding whether to drop a player?*

Jo-Jo: *That's easy: I check which free agent scored the most fantasy points the previous game. Then I pick him up and drop my worst player.*

Me: *And how do you identify your worst player?*

Jo-Jo: *That's easy again. Whichever guy is projected to do the worst that week, or maybe for the whole season, that's who I drop.*

Me: *Based on your projections?*

Jo-Jo: *Of course not. Who has time for that? I go off of what my league's website tells me.*

Are sirens blaring in your brain? It is *always* the right time to drop a player if a free agent is projected to score more fantasy points in the upcoming game and the remaining season. These projections must be based on your own due diligence, *not* on a website that invests much less time on fantasy research than you should. Haphazardly dropping a guy to make room for a one-hit wonder is no way to run a team. If you are considering making such a move, do your homework first, including answering dozens of questions just like these:

- Why did that free agent suddenly break out? Was someone else injured? Did most of the stats come during end-of-game "garbage time" when the defense was easing up?
- What is his outlook for the coming week? Is he starting? How tough is the opposing team's defense?
- What do the team's local beat reporters say? Do they anticipate a repeat performance? Why or why not?

As you know by now, each week at each position, "mediocre" players rise to the occasion and produce *kick-ass* results. Based on the size of your bench, you might have a couple of mediocre players riding the pine, serving as backups to your backups. Many await fantasy owners' favorable attention when the moment is right. On the other hand, when it comes to true middling talent, lightning rarely strikes twice in a row. A player's one-time greatness is not a prelude to further prominence unless various factors—including playing time, offensive scheme, quality of opponent, etc.— foretell long-term excellence.

In Week 1 of the 2007 season, Titans RB Chris Brown ran for 175 yards on 19 carries. Managers who had drafted him thought they had a weekly fantasy starter on their hands. In leagues where he was a free agent, managers clamored to add and start him in Week 2. Did these latter fantasy owners analyze whether Brown's short- and long-term fantasy value was greater than the player they cut to make room for him? Or were they so anxious to find the "next big thing" that they did what Jo-Jo does: drop their supposedly lowest-scoring player for a guy whose true strengths and weaknesses had not been accurately measured.

I made this careful assessment in my CBSSports league, where Brown was a free agent during Week 1. This solid RB was remarkable in an injury-plagued 2004 season and ran decently in 2005. But this was a new year with new variables to weigh. The former starter now was splitting carries with highly regarded second-year RB LenDale White, with highly touted run-focused rookie QB Vince Young expected to begin contributing at some point during the season. White and Young represented the team's future. At best Brown was a #3 RB with limited long-term fantasy upside—a terrific football player who, due to a more competitive backfield, was in danger of becoming an expendable fantasy option.

Brown competed in 11 more regular season games that year, scoring five times yet never topping 12 carries or 46 rushing yards. Most Jo-Jos who grabbed him based on his opening game stat line failed to comprehend his limitations, and also failed to recognize that the player they had to drop might have been a better fantasy option after all. They also did not know when to cut Brown, as many people held on to him for weeks, hoping to squeeze another brilliant effort out of him, while Brown rewarded them with two fantasy points, then four, then eight, then back to two, and so on. After analyzing the many reasons for a player's great performance, if little potential exists for a repeat performance, then why keep him on your team?

The Chris Brown example plays out nearly every week of every season. They are not hard to spot if you, like Dirk, are willing to scrutinize each breakout effort and assign a probability of continued success. When cavalierly dropping a player to make room for a perceived upgrade, you run the risk of abandoning an athlete who could have helped your team much more during the season. Only due diligence—

time and effort—will preserve your top talent, and in so doing, preserve your sanity.

As suggested in Chapter 11, I draft as many top-tier players as possible. These athletes tend to be the cream of the fantasy crop at their position. Meanwhile, second-tier players generally make valuable starters, third-tier players occasionally are valuable starters, and fourth-tier players are more in line with the "mediocre" talent who are useful a few times per season. In the next few paragraphs, my draft strategy will make even more sense with respect to dropping guys throughout the season.

Assuming a 12-player team that includes four bench spots, here are three draft scenarios. Which one would you choose for your fantasy team?

Draft Scenarios

	Option 1	Option 2	Option 3
Top-Tier Players	4	2	2
2nd-Tier Players	1	5	4
3rd-Tier Players	2	3	6
4th-Tier Players	5	2	0

Some people prefer Option 2 because it has seven players among the top two tiers—more than any other option. Others prefer Option 3 because, despite having one less second-tier player than Option 2, it includes a lot more third-tier players, and none of those "wasted" fourth-tier players.

One hundred times out of 100, I strive for Option 1. Mediocrity at the bottom of my roster does not faze me at all. What I care about most is recruiting a top-heavy lineup with as many positional point leaders as possible, because I trust that during the season I will locate and acquire more second- and third-tier players than my opponents, as I will work harder and smarter than anyone. In the meantime, my fourth-tier players are most valuable as occasional one-week fill-ins when circumstances warrant. And when a more promising player comes along, I rarely wonder whom I can afford to drop. Every day I know which player is my team's weakest link, which one is the next weakest, and which one is the weakest after that. Maintaining such a rank-order in my mind helps me expedite roster moves after I have identified better free agent talent.

Use your readily droppable players to hurt your opponents. Before Week 10 of the 2010 season, one of my friends competing in a separate league dropped a fourth-tier WR to pick up the Buccaneers DST—not because he needed a positional upgrade, but because his upcoming opponent's #1 DST was on a bye. The opponent had no need for the fourth-tier WR my friend discarded, and now had to choose among a sparser selection of available DSTs. The opponent's replacement DST performed very poorly that next week; he could have used the Bucs, which scored the ninth most fantasy points among DSTs that week. My friend won that week. But had he clung to his less valuable WR instead of engineering a one-week defensive block, he might have lost.

You can even adopt this blocking strategy to sabotage an opponent multiple weeks in advance. For example, suppose your record is 5-3. In two weeks you will compete against your co-worker, Jimmy, who also is 5-3 and whose stud QB will be on a bye when you meet. Jimmy does not have a backup QB because he has not yet thought about Week 10, which is a rather pathetic way to manage a fantasy team.

After a quick yet comprehensive analysis of Week 10 QB options, you cut three low-tier bench players that you anticipate not needing in the future in exchange for the top three prospective Week 10 QB performers: a third-tier player and two fourth-tier players. Only fourth- and fifth-tier QBs remain on waivers. Instead of letting him select a potential 15-point QB, you are forcing him to settle for a player who might garner seven to 10 points. You lose almost nothing by discarding your lower-tier talent, while simultaneously setting him back about five to eight points in your looming head-to-head matchup.

The playoffs are an ideal time to exploit opponents' roster weaknesses. A couple of weeks before the postseason begins, analyze potential matchups and begin targeting players most likely to improve their lineups. At which position are your anticipated opponents thinnest? You should have at least two droppable players at your disposal depending on bench size. Prevent your likely competitors from upgrading by exchanging your free agent fodder for the players most valuable to your prospective foes.

Some of the most effective player drops require mastery of intra-week timing. After uneven trades (e.g. 2-for-1), sometimes I am the one holding the extra player. By waiting until the last possible instant to discard that player (e.g. right before the week's first kickoff), I successfully prevent competitors from claiming him. He might have filled a short-term hole in a competitor's lineup. Instead he helps no one, thereby helping me.

At other times I might possess a "weak link" at a particular position (generally a TE, K, or DST) that is no better than a third- or fourth-tier weekly performer—easily replaceable. At each week's earliest possible moment, I drop that player in exchange for someone my upcoming opponent needs most. Then at the week's last possible moment, I release him for the player I dropped earlier. In the rare instance when my third-tier castoff has been claimed, I simply add a different player from that position with the highest probability of scoring the most fantasy points that week. As a result, I have lost essentially nothing while limiting my forthcoming opponent's fantasy point potential.

You might be asking, "If your opponent wants that third-tier player so much, why don't you keep him?" The answer: Drop whomever you need to drop to improve your chances for victory. If an opponent wants my starting K, and if I value two other free agent Ks equally, then I have everything to gain by dropping my K, blocking my opponent from adding a player who would *really* help him, and then later adding a replacement K of comparable fantasy scoring prowess.

Here is another example: Suppose my opponent in the preceding scenario needs an RB because his usual starting #2 RB is on a bye or is hurt or has been demoted. I want to block him from adding the free agent RB with the highest likelihood for the most fantasy points *this week*. That target might be a sixth-tier RB who, due to several favorable circumstances, is primed for fourth-tier production this week, making him the most valuable waiver prize. But if this sixth-tier RB's *long-term* prospects (after this next game) are dim, and if I already start a first-tier RB and third-tier RB with a fifth-tier RB riding my bench, then why would I need an inferior reserve at that position? However, if this #6 RB is likely to produce more short- *and* long-term fantasy points than my #5 RB, then a swap absolutely is merited.

As for player demotions, such shifts do not necessarily affect long-term value. Some players are demoted for a game or two to teach them a lesson / set their head straight / help them get healthier before rejoining the starting lineup. Sometimes a promising backup proves to be less effective than the former starter. By following the news and anticipating NFL depth chart decisions, you can seize on opponents' fears through trades and snatch second- or third-tier players at their lowest value. But if you discover a shift in future value, whereby your recently demoted player—or any of your players, for that matter—are no longer as valuable as a particular free agent, then you know what to do: cut him loose.

Too many Jo-Jos are obsessed with their fantasy stars, overlooking how the shrewdest and most effective maneuvers often entail seemingly subtle roster and lineup shifts. Day after day you have more control over tiny victories (like blocking an opponent from upgrading his TE) than big paydays (like identifying and starting an undervalued fantasy stud). When you find a big payday through meticulous research, cherish it. You deserve it. But as noted earlier, many head-to-head battles are decided by only a handful of points. On which side of that equation will you be? *Always* contemplate ways to boost your next score—and limit your opponent's—even by a single point. By investing time and resources on which players to drop and when, you will continually maximize fantasy output while minimizing that of your upcoming opponents.

CHAPTER 18

INJURIES = OPPORTUNITIES

"A quick temper will make a fool of you soon enough."
– Bruce Lee

The Parable of the Good Samaritan Running Back

A certain running back went down from head to turf, and fell among linebackers, who stripped him of his ball, and wounded him, and returned to their huddle, leaving him out six to eight weeks.

And by chance there came down that way a certain backup running back; and when he saw the wounded first-stringer, he passed by on the other side, joined his huddle, and proceeded to rush for 60 yards on 11 carries and a score.

The biggest complaint I hear from fantasy friends and adversaries alike is, "Poor me. My best players are hurt. I'm so unlucky." Not that I am insensitive to others' plight. But these whiners blame everyone but themselves: "Somebody up there must hate me. I give up." It took three injuries in three weeks for a competitor in my current NBA fantasy league to quit playing altogether; his ailing starting lineup has remained unchanged to this day, while he has ignored dozens of game-changing free agents that have boosted the rest of the league's teams, and which would have made him a contender if he had Dirk's convictions.

You might know people like this young man. You might have been one yourself in a former life, before reading this book. Such sorry saps fail to see the birds beyond the smokestacks, the sunshine through the clouds, and the sky through their bedroom wall after they have punched a hole through it.

During the 2007 NFL season, amidst my blogging days, Rudi Johnson got hurt. In addition to being the Bengals' stalwart RB for several seasons, he was a fantasy stud with the following track record:

Rudi Johnson Rushing Statistics (2004-2006)

	Rushing Yards	TDs
2004	1,454	12
2005	1,458	12
2006	1,309	12

Entering 2007 Johnson was a (nearly) can't-miss first or early second round draft selection. When he went down in Week 3, nearly every manager who had him alternately cried, kicked, and vomited in agony. However, a few of us viewed Johnson not as a fantasy failure, but as a Good Samaritan bringing joy to all those seeking another good RB. In this case, the reward was Kenny Watson.

A 29-year-old with six career starts, Watson took 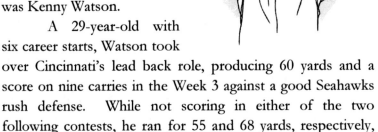 over Cincinnati's lead back role, producing 60 yards and a score on nine carries in the Week 3 against a good Seahawks rush defense. While not scoring in either of the two following contests, he ran for 55 and 68 yards, respectively, on 13 rushes apiece, including against a comparably tough

Patriots rush defense. From an NFL perspective, he had exhibited great poise and ability by averaging 5.23 yards per carry against stiff competition. Yet from a fantasy perspective, he had garnered only five to seven points per game, which is why no one claimed him after weeks 3, 4, 5, or 6. After Johnson returned for a few snaps in Week 6 and was listed as "questionable" heading into Week 7, it appeared Watson's modest contributions were nearing an end.

But I refused to abandon Watson. The Bengals next played at home against the Jets, which owned one of the weakest rush defenses in the league. Although he had scored only once since assuming starting duties, I long believed (and still do) that for RBs who run well in an offense that knows how to score, the TDs will come eventually. Watson's poor fantasy numbers were not for lack of talent, but because the Bengals had relied heavily on their passing game recently, as they frequently had played from behind during their last three games (which also happened to be losses). Facing a weaker Week 7 opponent, Cincinnati would give space—and the Jets would yield space—to whoever started at RB. My extensive research reinforced this theory.

When Johnson's condition dropped to "doubtful" on Friday, I immediately picked up Watson and dropped an expendable player. On my blog I publicly predicted that Watson would be the #1 undervalued RB performer of the week, making him the top free agent RB pickup to start in Week 7. I explained my reasoning and urged everyone within Internet range to add and activate him.

The result: Watson rushed 31 times for 130 yards and three TDs that Sunday, and also caught three passes for 27 yards. He *was* Cincinnati's offense that day, as the coaching staff let him pound the Jets' anemic rush defense into submission. Unheralded by prognosticators far and wide, Watson nevertheless scored the most fantasy points among all RBs that week.

To those of you hoping to improve your teams (i.e. all of you), commit to memory the Parable of the Good Samaritan Running Back. It plays out week after week, season after season. One player's injury can be another player's bust-out performance. By selecting the correct replacement early and often, you will win. Simple? No. But that is why I am here.

Remember, fantasy football is 25% draft, 25% drops/adds, 25% starts/sits, and 25% luck. Bad luck happens. For *kick-ass* fantasy competitors, good luck happens far more often. Why? Because we see the good in every bad situation. Sometimes an injury paves the way for acquiring someone of roughly equal—and occasionally greater—value. Similarly, every demotion means a recently undervalued player now gets a shot at fantasy greatness, while every coaching strategy change (e.g. from a run-heavy to a pass-heavy offensive) might hurt your RB today, but it will help your soon-to-be-acquired TE and WR next week. While not always seeking changing circumstances, we must continually embrace them in order to thrive.

Heading into the 2010 season, few people outside of San Diego had heard of WR Seyi Ajirotutu. Led by QB Philip Rivers, TE Antonio Gates, and WR Vincent Jackson, the Chargers' passing game was expected to be a boon for fantasy owners. By Week 9, however, the Chargers had lost top receivers Jackson, Gates, and WR Malcolm Floyd to injuries. Occasionally valuable WR Legedu Naanee also was out. That meant for Week 9's contest, 31-year-old journeymen Patrick Crayton and Randy McMichael became the team's #1 WR and #1 TE, respectively, while Ajirotutu was assigned to the #2 WR slot. Ajirotutu had five receptions for 74 yards in the previous two games—the only two games of his young NFL career.

Most fantasy managers who had Gates, Jackson, Floyd, and even a healthy Rivers on their team sunk into a deep depression. Surely the squad's heralded passing game would be kept at bay without their star players. Dirk, however, understood the implications of seemingly devastating injuries:

- The Chargers' Week 9 opponent, the Texans, had the second worst pass defense in the league.
- No team had given up more fantasy points to WRs than the Texans.
- Facing Houston's explosive offense, led by top-flight WR Andre Johnson and #1 RB Arian Foster, San Diego might have to go airborne to keep up.

At the week's outset, two of the three "mediocre" players expected to play big roles—McMichael and Ajirotutu—were available in my league. Unfortunately the limits of a two-player bench prevented me from overhauling my roster, as I could afford to add and start only one player. After all, the Chargers' first-stringers were expected back soon, so it would have been stupid to surrender my long-term contributors for multiple one- or two-week substitutes. With a deeper bench, however, I would have grabbed both guys, as well as Crayton if he had been available.

So I initially claimed Ajirotutu off waivers and dropped my only expendable player. Then a competitor surprisingly dumped Crayton. Why? Who cares. I knew more than he did. With no roster flexibility, I resignedly dropped Ajirotutu and claimed Crayton, believing that the latter's extensive experience would prevail over Ajirotutu's untested potential. And anyway, in the Chargers' previous three games, Crayton had averaged 5.4 catches and 82 yards.

The power of *mediocrity* was on full display that week, as Ajirotutu caught four balls for 111 yards and two TDs, while McMichael caught two passes for 23 yards and two

TDs. These would be their only scores all season, as neither player made even a remote fantasy impact the rest of the year. Their power lay in the misery of others, and they filled in more admirably than most people (me excluded) anticipated. And I prevailed that week despite Crayton's mild showing (three catches for 70 yards), as my team was led by Arian Foster's 197 total yards and two TDs, as well as Terrell Owens' 10 catches for 141 yards and two TDs (leading all WRs in fantasy scoring that week). Again, with sufficient roster flexibility I would have added all three players—as much for my own benefit as to keep them out of other smart owners' hands. Today I continue using this strategy to great effect: hunting for injured players' replacements, analyzing their probability of success, and reaping the benefits.

Update your player matrix to reflect injury news and depth chart shifts. By searching hard and wide enough, you will find at least one viable injury replacement each week. Most of these players should be available in your league. If you carry a sizable bench, learn how to anticipate the impact of future fantasy fill-ins by projecting several weeks ahead. If one team's stud #1 WR and solid #2 WR are playing hurt, and you have no better options at the moment, pick up that team's #3 and #4 WRs. If either top WR misses time down the road, you are in a better position for a Watson-esque or Ajirotutu-esque breakout.

Injuries are not a time for tears; they are a time for roster upgrades. One fantasy owner's curse can be your blessing.

CHAPTER 19

THE REBOUND EFFECT

(A.K.A. THE *KICK-ASS* LAW OF AVERAGES)

"Study the past if you would divine the future."
– Confucius

With the possible exception of unknown greatness residing in untapped corners of the globe, professional athletes are the world's most talented in their respective sport. I recently hit a few ping-pong balls with Sanil Shetty, one of the top three table tennis players in India. Having played ping-pong since the age of six, I had never felt intimidated by *anyone* on the other side of the net . . . until meeting Shetty. Compared to me, his talent is immeasurable. And later, as he hit balls with his coach—with the speed and accuracy of a machine—I observed a consistency that I could never hope to match in this game.

The same can be said for any sport. I also play basketball recreationally. Some days my shot goes in, while other days it does not. But if I observed Kevin Durant doing shooting drills with his coach, the NBA superstar's shot would be vastly more consistent. Compared to me, and against some of the planet's stiffest competition (as opposed to the fellow scrubs I play against), Durant makes a higher percentage of shots, shoots fewer air balls, makes better passes, plays better defense, sets better screens, grabs more rebounds, has better court vision, and so on. The list is as endless as what one can do on a basketball court.

When facing extraordinarily talented opponents night after night, any great player is susceptible to "off games." But an off night for Shetty or Durant or any other athletic icon would equate to the greatest sports performance of my life.

If instead of Jean van de Velde, it had been *me* protecting a three-shot lead on the final hole of the 1999 British Open, I would have taken a seven in a heartbeat and laughed all the way to an inevitable playoff defeat.

Great players do great things with great consistency. A sport's greatest players are even more consistent. Bad games usually are offset by many more good and great games. That is what it means to be an elite talent: While one might be stymied in any given contest, superior ability is held in check for only so long. This is due partly to skill, partly to work ethic (making adjustments), and partly to heart (wanting to be the best). I call this propensity for peak performers to bounce back "the rebound effect."

The fantasy implications are nuanced, as this tool is harder to quantify than those presented earlier. But that does not prevent us from assigning probabilities for players' future performance based on their skill level and previous game's production.

Over the years I have observed that when a relatively poor performer endures a bad game, he is not likely to rebound in his next contest. As a perennially limited fantasy producer, his capacity to rebound is curbed by numerous factors including where he sits on his team's depth chart, strength of upcoming opposing defense, etc. When a *mediocre* competitor plays poorly, he possesses a mediocre chance of rebounding in his next contest. Once again, his ability to bounce back hinges on dozens of criteria, including those just mentioned.

But in general (i.e. not always, but frequently enough to integrate with our *kick-ass* philosophy), when a great player suffers an off night, we immediately can assign some probability that this athlete will rebound to his customary (or sometimes even higher) production level in his next game. This probability rises or falls based on numerous factors including number of touches per game, scoring opportunities, injury concerns, player insights ("Coach wanted me to be a decoy today to draw double-teams, so that's what I was."), and any other information that could impact future performance. When poor play is not due to physical, mental, or long-term strategic factors, then one's rebound potential increases.

To examine this scenario more thoroughly, here is a hypothetical example: CB (Cornerback) A and WR B compete in the same division on teams with the same win-loss record. CB A is one of the top CB's in the NFL. WR B is a #2 WR in your league—not elite, but essentially startable every week. Playing on the road in Week 7, CB A's team was crushed, as he and his safeties were burned by WR B for 12 catches, 135 yards, and two TDs. This was CB A's worst performance of the year. And your research demonstrates that CB A is (a) not at an age when skill level begins to decline, (b) injury free, and (c) pissed.

Now it is Week 12, and these two teams are set to play again, this time on CB A's home turf. When analyzing the circumstances that led to Week 7's outcome, and assuming all other factors are equal, I will always lean toward CB A and his team exacting sweet revenge against WR B when they face off in Week 12. Why? Because there was nothing inherently wrong with CB A five weeks earlier; he and his teammates simply were outplayed or outcoached. CB A is not accustomed to taking such a beating. He is gifted, healthy, and now has a chip on his shoulder. Unlike WR B, he is an elite positional talent.

In addition, any defensive coordinator worth his weight in salary will develop a scheme to ensure that WR B does not beat them again. Yes, WR B is good. But when considering whether to start WR B the second time around, understand the risks, as the *rebound effect* dictates that the odds are against WR B from duplicating his prior brilliance, while

CB A and his teammates are more likely to make adjustments and shut him down.

Before making any decisions, learn how CB A, WR B, and their respective teams are preparing for the rematch. Remember, the *rebound effect* is not automatic; it is one of several factors we use to assign probabilities for future performance. If CB A is slowed by a hamstring injury, or if WR B has become a more dangerous and multidimensional offensive weapon since Week 7, then adjust your probabilities accordingly. However, barring such shifting conditions, be aware that dozens of free agent WRs might post more fantasy points than WR B in Week 12. I know, because I have repeatedly witnessed unclaimed players achieve sporadic stardom, and have enjoyed incredible fantasy success by capitalizing on the relative predictability of their impending statistical explosion.

So be smart. If not slowed by injuries, holdouts, suspensions, or other game-changing factors, most elite fantasy players—however poorly they perform here and there—will enjoy terrific seasons at levels at or near your preseason projections. How? By frequently following bad games with great ones. They fall and rise based on the law of averages. While Sanil Shetty and Kevin Durant endure off nights, barring injuries or mental breakdowns, they are quite likely to recover and return to greatness in their next contest—and if not that one, then the one after that. The point is that a certain probability exists for rebounding, because at their current skill level compared to competitors, most elite talent will thrive over the course of a season.

This theory applies to *mediocre* players as well, but in a slightly different way. Entering the 2007 season, 29-year-old WR Kevin Curtis's career numbers included 136 receptions, 1,714 receiving yards, and 12 TDs. In his first year with the Philadelphia Eagles, Curtis entered Week 1 as a #4 or #5 WR in most fantasy leagues—a mediocre player possessing the potential for a few good games, depending on how his rapport developed with QB Donovan McNabb, the health and abilities of the Eagles' other receivers, and the coaching staff's weekly game plan. After two quiet games to start the season, Curtis broke out in Week 3 with 221 receiving yards and three TDs against the Lions. Such gaudy stats usually are reserved for the NFL's most elite players, perhaps only once or twice in their lifetime.

So what happened next? Of course you know the answer. Most of the world's Jo-Jos clamored to pick him up, suddenly making this perpetually mediocre WR the hottest commodity on waivers. Heading into his Week 3 contest, Curtis was a starter in only 9% of all CBSSports fantasy leagues. Heading into Week 4, that number rose to 80%.

80%.

Curtis was a late bloomer in the NFL—a rarity among high-impact fantasy players, and for good reason. He turned 25 before playing in his first game and caught his first TD pass at age 26. Before busting out in Week 3 of the 2007 season, he had enjoyed only one career 100-yard receiving game. Who was the real Kevin Curtis? Did he deserve to be owned in only 9% of fantasy leagues? That probably was selling him short, as during that offseason Philadelphia had signed him to a six-year, $32 million contract with financial incentives, whereupon the team's general manager, Tom Heckert, announced that Curtis had a "real good chance to be a starter" (*Philadelphia Inquirer*, 3/16/07). But did he deserve to be owned in 80% of CBSSports fantasy leagues? That is where our homework pays off. I went on a mission to learn what the team's coaches were saying about Curtis's surprising performance. I read the hometown newspapers to learn what the local beat reporters knew. I analyzed every conceivable condition that made this outburst possible:

- The Eagles' coaches and players were very disappointed after starting the season a surprising 0-2.
- The Lions had an atrocious pass defense (they went on to yield 4,131 receiving yards in 2007—second most in the NFL).
- Philadelphia's 2007 receiving corps was almost a mirror image of the one that took the field each week in 2006, and included elite weapon RB Brian Westbrook, who in addition to his rushing prowess also accumulated 699 receiving yards and four receiving TDs.
- In a very similar Eagles system in 2006, Donte Stallworth—a mediocre talent with occasional starting potential—averaged about 60 receiving yards and half of a TD per game.

Curtis would not play many more bad pass defenses that season. In addition, the Eagles had numerous offensive weapons, meaning Curtis was not a focal point like most elite WRs; in fact, his statistical apex was closer to the man he replaced (Stallworth) than a generic #1 WR.

I concluded that Curtis's value was higher than the 9% ownership witnessed before Week 3, but much lower than the 80% ownership bestowed upon him before Week 4. In my CBSSports league, he was added right after his Week 3 performance, then dropped after his somewhat predictable Week 4 *rebound* (two receptions for 21 yards and zero TDs), then added again *after* he scored another TD in Week 6, then dropped again after Week 12, having gone scoreless during that six-week stretch.

My opponents held Curtis for seven games that season, during which he averaged only five fantasy points per contest. He was a free agent during his four best games, when he amassed 40, 18, 17, and 13 fantasy points, respectively. In other words, my opponents failed to accurately measure Curtis's fantasy potential week to week. And based on his constantly fluctuating ownership in all CBSSports leagues throughout the year, many other managers misread his value, too.

Curtis was an otherwise valuable *mediocre* player (per Chapter 3) who most people mistakenly branded as a fantasy stud. He hurt many teams that he deserved to help, simply because too many managers misread his potential and were too lazy or incapable of acquiring all of the facts. The reality is that about 25% of the time, Curtis served as a terrific bye week replacement, particularly in Week 3, when one might have predicted a fantasy point uptick based on the opposition's porous defense, and then again in the all-important (fantasy playoff relevant) Week 16 versus the equally awful Saints pass defense. As we have already learned, mediocrity thrives at various times throughout each season. Through diligent investigation, we discover when mediocre players like Kevin Curtis are primed for breakout performances.

Likewise, we can apply the *rebound effect* to mediocre players, concluding that these occasional rock stars rarely follow a big game with another big game. If they regularly did, then they no longer would be mediocre players. But the law of averages dictates that *most* mediocre players, despite occasionally inspiring fantasy outbursts, are unable to sustain such numbers. Curtis followed each of his double-digit fantasy point efforts with two points, than six, then two, and then six again. Other mediocre players mentioned in this book—including QB Chad Pennington, RB Chris Brown, and WR Seyi Ajirotutu—experienced similar fates.

I challenge you to test the *rebound effect* on any mediocre player. Most of the time, any player you have accurately identified as *mediocre* will follow any big game with a relative clunker. There are many reasons why: the next team's defense comes prepared to stifle him; the player's offensive scheme reverts to leaning on the team's best players; and so on. One *kick-ass* performance does not translate into a full season of *kick-ass* performances. By anticipating when mediocre players will fall back down to Earth—through the natural law of rebounding—you will be another step closer to dominating your league.

During draft prep and the chapter on *taking*, we tested fantasy football hypotheses to expand our knowledge and improve our ability to predict future fantasy outcomes. You are now armed with a framework for analyzing and refining numerous hypotheses governing player/positional performance. So let's examine two new hypotheses that, while not corresponding directly to individual rebounds like those highlighted above, do shed light on how some of the NFL's best players—and even some mediocre ones—have rebounded after a *team* loss.

Post-Loss Advantage

Do the NFL's best positional players score more fantasy points after a loss than after other game results?

I have long surmised that a majority of great NFL athletes hate to lose: not a bold statement by any stretch, yet worth establishing as a starting point for future study. So when a team is defeated, to what extent do their elite players "rise to the occasion" in their next game? And by extension, with what regularity should fantasy managers anticipate a boost in these players' fantasy point totals in that post-loss contest?

From 2008 to 2010, for the top 20 players at each position, I tracked their fantasy point production in each game immediately following a loss versus all other results (after a win, after a tie, and to start the season in Week 1). To maintain consistency, I used the same fantasy points system (one point per 40 passing yards, one point per 10 rushing yards, one point per 10 receiving yards, six points per TD, minus two points per offensive turnover, two points per defensive turnover, one point per extra point, minus three points per missed extra point, etc.). And as usual, I excluded all stats from the final two games of each regular season, during which some playoff-bound teams rest their best players, while some other teams are inclined to rest or limit star players who normally would play, but who need not risk further injury for relatively meaningless games.

The following table shows that during this three-year period, the top 20 players per position averaged 0.61 more fantasy points after a loss than after any other result. RBs owned the largest advantage, while TEs were only negligibly more productive after a team loss:

Top 20 Players per Position: Post-Loss Fantasy Points Advantage

	QB	RB	WR	TE	K	DST	Avg Fantasy Point Differential
2008	1.15	-0.96	-1.02	0.47	0.90	0.64	0.20
2009	0.44	1.04	2.84	-1.49	1.06	0.63	0.75
2010	0.04	2.97	0.07	1.05	0.35	0.80	0.88
Avg Fantasy Point Differential	**0.54**	**1.02**	**0.63**	**0.01**	**0.77**	**0.69**	**0.61**

Then I narrowed the analysis to include only the top *10* players per position, as I wondered whether more elite positional talent rebounded from a team loss particularly well, and therefore distinguished themselves from slightly lower-tier players. This theory turned out to be statistically valid, as the average post-loss fantasy advantage of all positional top

10 players combined was larger across all three seasons. Competing after a loss clearly benefitted WRs and DSTs, while QBs and TEs lagged:

Top 10 Players per Position:
Post-Loss Fantasy Points Advantage

	QB	RB	WR	TE	K	DST	Avg Fantasy Point Differential
2008	1.74	-1.49	-0.76	0.79	1.34	1.29	**0.48**
2009	0.45	1.31	2.78	-1.76	0.66	2.87	**1.05**
2010	-1.94	2.26	2.77	1.13	1.14	1.40	**1.13**
Avg Fantasy Point Differential	**0.08**	**0.69**	**1.59**	**0.05**	**1.05**	**1.85**	**0.89**

Overall, we identify a solid benefit to starting most position players coming off a loss. Incorporating these findings into your daily roster decisions midseason probably won't turn a 2-5 team into an 8-5 playoff-bound team. So please don't throw this book out the window thinking you have all the answers. (And really, for safety reasons, don't throw books period.) This one belongs in your hands on the train every morning, inspiring other commuters to buy it for Christmas, Hanukkah, Kwanzaa, or their grandma's birthday.

Now let's make more sense of these numbers by plugging them into a fantasy lineup that we have used throughout this book: one QB, two RBs, two WRs, one TE, one K, and one DST. Assuming each member of your lineup is a top 20 positional player, collectively the lineup would have averaged a modest 5.30 more fantasy points in post-loss contests than in other games:

Top 20 Players per Position:
Post-Loss Fantasy Points Advantage (Starting Lineup)

	QB	2 RBs	2 WRs	TE	K	DST	Lineup Fantasy Point Differential
2008	1.15	-1.92	-2.03	0.47	0.90	0.64	-0.78
2009	0.44	2.07	5.69	-1.49	1.06	0.63	8.39
2010	0.04	5.94	0.13	1.05	0.35	0.80	8.31
Lineup Fantasy Point Differential	0.54	2.03	1.26	0.01	0.77	0.69	5.30

Suppose you are a gifted fantasologist whose lineup includes only top *10* players at each position. By halving the size of your player pool to accommodate only elite fantasy scorers, your lineup collectively would have averaged 7.61 more fantasy points in post-loss games versus other contests:

Top 10 Players per Position:
Post-Loss Fantasy Points Advantage (Starting Lineup)

	QB	2 RBs	2 WRs	TE	K	DST	Lineup Fantasy Point Differential
2008	1.74	-2.99	-1.52	0.79	1.34	1.29	0.65
2009	0.45	2.62	5.56	-1.76	0.66	2.87	10.40
2010	-1.94	4.52	5.53	1.13	1.14	1.40	11.79
Lineup Fantasy Point Differential	0.08	1.39	3.19	0.05	1.05	1.85	7.61

In conclusion, top 10 WRs, TEs, Ks, and DSTs would have helped your team after a loss more than their 11th-to-20th ranked counterparts. On the flip side, the 11th to 20th best QBs and RBs averaged comparatively more post-loss fantasy points than their top 10 brethren. Whether due to athletes' competitiveness, coaches' shifting strategies, and/or other post-loss factors, we observe a clear statistical advantage among most of the 120 players studied each season.

Why are these results meaningful? Regardless of draft position or waiver system, your lineup primarily should consist of top 20 players at each position, with allowances for a #3 RB and/or #3 WR if rules require playing one or both of them, or other mediocre players outside the top 20 when research reveals a high probability of success. Unless competing in a 20+ team league, if you are saddled with numerous players ranked 21st to 30th at their position, then re-read my three earlier chapters on *fielding/finding a league you can dominate, drafting,* and *taking.* And stop sobbing.

We have just learned that between 2008 and 2010, the NFL's best positional players scored more fantasy points rebounding from a loss than after all other game results. And since your lineup is loaded with top 20 positional players, if these results reflect an annual trend, then you might be able to generate several extra fantasy points per week by tracking which if your players are coming off a defeat.

As you know by now, this does *not* mean that you should *solely* start players coming off a loss. This strategy is one of many presented in this book and should be applied in conjunction with the rest. For example, we have already deduced that during this three-year period, top 20 players score more fantasy points at home than on the road. So if you are weighing which of two top 10 DSTs to start in a particular week, if one is playing at home (0.86-point edge versus road games) *and* after a loss (1.85-point edge), and the other is playing away after a win, and if all other factors essentially are equal, then increase your potential production and pick the DST playing at home after a loss

This example raises a new question—one whose quantitative answer could yield even more bankable information for our fantasy teams.

One-Game Losing Streak Home Field Advantage

Do the NFL's best positional players score more fantasy points when playing at home while trying to snap a one-game losing streak, as opposed to all other game scenarios?

This is what we know: Between 2008 and 2010, top 20 positional players averaged more fantasy points at home than away, while also averaging more fantasy points in games after a loss than after a win, tie, or to start the season. Each trend garners modest fantasy returns. So what happens when we almost merge these two useful concepts into one uber-hypothesis?

From 2008 to 2010, for the top 20 players at each position, I measured their fantasy point production for all home games that took place while their team was in the midst of a mere one-game losing streak, versus all other game scenarios. I postulated that players would be more likely to rebound at home after a single loss than after a victory or a prolonged winless streak. While this specific reasoning was not analyzed, it was the basis for narrowing this study's scope. To complete this study, I continued to use my standard fantasy points system. And as always, I did not include stats for the last two games of each regular season.

The following table highlights that, during this three-year period, each position's top 20 players collectively averaged 1.01 more fantasy points when playing at home during a one-game losing streak than during other contests. This advantage was relatively significant during each season and for each position:

Top 20 Players per Position: One-Game Losing Streak
Home Field Fantasy Points Advantage

	QB	RB	WR	TE	K	DST	Avg Fantasy Point Differential
2008	1.91	0.13	-0.45	1.19	0.28	2.93	**1.00**
2009	-1.18	2.99	2.68	-2.05	2.14	3.38	**1.33**
2010	1.27	0.29	1.05	2.10	0.53	-1.04	**0.70**
Avg Fantasy Point Differential	**0.67**	**1.14**	**1.09**	**0.41**	**0.98**	**1.76**	**1.01**

Now let's reduce our focus merely to the top 10 players at each position. Would this elite group have a greater propensity to excel in a home contest / one-game winless streak scenario? As we see below, the difference is rather remarkable. Except for QBs, all other elite-level positional players averaged more fantasy points than their 11th-to-20th ranked counterparts, as the statistical advantage of several positional categories skyrocketed when separated from the pack:

Top 10 Players per Position: One-Game Losing Streak
Home Field Fantasy Points Advantage

	QB	RB	WR	TE	K	DST	Avg Fantasy Point Differential
2008	3.09	1.33	-1.72	0.71	-0.51	4.66	**1.26**
2009	-2.75	6.72	2.84	-0.43	2.99	5.94	**2.55**
2010	-0.21	0.22	2.59	2.36	0.78	1.03	**1.13**
Avg Fantasy Point Differential	**0.05**	**2.76**	**1.24**	**0.88**	**1.09**	**3.88**	**1.65**

These findings should not surprise us; they are an amalgam of what we have already learned, with only a slight variance (*one-game losing streak* versus *post-loss*). We know that between 2008 and 2010, home teams won 56.72% of the time, while top 20 positional players averaged more fantasy points in home games and when competing after a defeat. When condensed into a somewhat unifying scenario, each trend's favorable tendencies became even more prominent. The results, therefore, are even more certifiable, further solidifying our strategic approach for winning fantasy football.

To quantify how these outcomes would have benefited your fantasy team (comprised of top 20 positional players) between 2008 and 2010, examine the following table:

Top 20 Players per Position: One-Game Losing Streak Home Field Fantasy Points Advantage (Starting Lineup)

	QB	2 RBs	2 WRs	TE	K	DST	Lineup Fantasy Point Differential
2008	1.91	0.25	-0.90	1.19	0.28	2.93	**5.67**
2009	-1.18	5.99	5.36	-2.05	2.14	3.38	**13.64**
2010	1.27	0.59	2.10	2.10	0.53	-1.04	**5.54**
Lineup Fantasy Point Differential	**0.67**	**2.28**	**2.19**	**0.41**	**0.98**	**1.76**	8.28

And what about for lineups comprised solely of elite-level (top 10) positional players?

Top 10 Players per Position: One-Game Losing Streak Home Field Fantasy Points Advantage (Starting Lineup)

	QB	2 RBs	2 WRs	TE	K	DST	Lineup Fantasy Point Differential
2008	3.09	2.66	-3.44	0.71	-0.51	4.66	**7.17**
2009	-2.75	13.44	5.68	-0.43	2.99	5.94	**24.88**
2010	-0.21	0.43	5.18	2.36	0.78	1.03	**9.56**
Lineup Fantasy Point Differential	0.05	5.51	2.47	0.88	1.09	3.88	**13.87**

Among the hypotheses we have tested thus far, this one yields the most useful/bankable results. While there are no guarantees that this three-season trend continues into the future, we have discovered the most concrete evidence yet of a fantasy principle that, if applied between 2008 and 2010, would have helped your team significantly.

*   *   *

As with any fantasy tool, the *rebounding effect* should not be applied in a vacuum. When combining multiple applicable scenarios, you might uncover more concrete evidence for accurately predicting player success, as well as further augmenting your weekly fantasy point totals.

Heed this lesson: Don't settle for a two-point advantage when, with additional study, you might earn a four-point advantage. Rather than embrace two distinct theories as separate entities, analyze whether, when joined, they produce a unified theory with even greater benefits. Keep searching. Keep testing. Keep reconstituting until your earned advantages no longer can be augmented.

CHAPTER 20

BYE

*"I'm just kind of taking a break now
and enjoying the freedom of making my own choices."*
– Andrew Shue

Now let's pause for a much-deserved breather—a break from thinking and eyeing and touching all things fantasy sports. Am I a softy? Hardly. I am just playing with what we are given. Each year you can count on three days when no NFL, MLB, NBA, or NHL games are played: the MLB All-Star break. After investing 50-60 hours per week at my craft, it is a little disconcerting to wake up one Monday morning each July to discover that there is nothing on my plate. It is too early to think seriously about football, too late to research basketball or hockey (whose seasons ended the previous month), and not entirely necessary to focus on baseball. Oh sure, I could spend the next 80 hours preparing for Thursday's matchups. But I prefer to welcome this respite as a sign from the fantasy gods.

I call this period my "bye."

You might be asking, "How do I behave like a normal member of society after being inundated with names, data, statistics, news stories, and other pressing matters during the past 360+ days?" Some of you martyrs might even be wondering, "Do I even *deserve* three days off?"

Everyone needs a battery recharge. Believe me, I would rather keep focusing on sports while most "real" players are on vacation. However, it is not healthy for anyone in the long run. We are only human. Taking a three-day break each year is vital for keeping our brain functioning at a peak level and ensuring future fantasy dominance.

Below is a list of my annual bye activities. May it inspire you as it has so many others:

DAY 1

Catch up on Movies, Television, and Current Events
Time: 18 hours

Watch the latest in entertainment and non-sports news, which might be fodder for a brilliant (but not stupid) team name while simultaneously distracting you from your stress-ridden fantasy world. I always select one season of a show that makes my wife laugh or cry—an emotive tool that stretches facial muscles and/or cleanses tear ducts. Then we check out four recent Oscar-winning films and the year's 10 most-viewed YouTube videos. Finally, we watch a three-hour summary of the previous 12 months of CBS Evening News, which my spouse has lovingly cobbled together each night after I have gone to sleep.

DAY 2

Read Books
Time: 16 hours

Fiction or non-fiction? I splurge and buy one of each: well-reviewed tomes on the *New York Times* bestseller list. I am a slow (i.e. careful) reader, so I choose books that are under 150 pages, have plenty of dialogue and indented bullet points, and contain many pictures, illustrations, and blank pages separating chapters.

Nap
Time: two hours

A two-hour nap leaves me alert and refreshed. I don't have time to wedge in quick snoozes during the fantasy year, except under my desk at work.

DAY 3

Meditate
Time: one hour

After a year on the go (if not physically, then always mentally), I restore balance to mind, body, and soul. Think nothing. Desire nothing. Be nothing. Scratch nothing.

Bathe
Time: two hours

I run a scalding hot tub full of water, add at least seven distinct brands of massage oils, toss in Mr. Bubble, and stir for 10 minutes with a cooking whisk. Once submerged, I visualize the end-of-fantasy-season victory banquet, when all vanquished friends and foes will join me in celebration, gazing upon me with envy and admiration.

Call Family and Friends
Time: one hour

You probably have not spoken with close friends or family for several months, and perhaps for almost a year if you are a year-round fantasy participant. So take out your phone and briefly re-enter their lives. For maximum efficiency, make it a conference call with everyone. No need to divulge your doings, since surely they already know, given your routine absence from all non-fantasy-related activities like weddings, funerals, and folk concerts. They will appreciate your willingness to sacrifice several minutes of your busy life to listen somewhat.

Cook a Meal
Time: one hour

After weeks of pampering by your partner and/or children, it is time to return the favor via the kitchen. Whether you prepare something simple (spaghetti) or much more complex (spaghetti with sauce), they will not soon forget such exceptional kindness. And if you don't have any family, enjoy cooking for yourself. You deserve it. Just this once.

Back up Your Computer
Time: two hours and 30 minutes

In the midst of writing this book, my laptop motherboard crashed. (It really did.) My computer contained bookmarks for the world's most comprehensive and accurate fantasy websites. In addition to this manuscript, there were Excel and Word files containing years upon years of *kick-ass* statistics—the lifeblood of my fantasy fortune. Thankfully, a resourceful computer specialist salvaged everything. The insightful analysis presented in this book was not lost to history because of one extraordinary man whose name currently escapes me.

Back up your computer often. You have worked too hard to let technical breakdowns hinder your fantasological progress. But once a year, go one step further: e-mail all fantasy-related bookmarks and files to yourself. Then download them onto two newly purchased external hard drives; deliver one to your safe deposit box downtown and bury the other in your backyard. If you don't have a backyard, then bury it in a nearby forest.

Stock up on Groceries
Time: three hours

My wife, housekeeper, and French gardener keep my family's refrigerator filled. Yet why must its contents be so disgustingly healthy? To prepare for the year ahead, I rent a U-Haul and drive to the nearby super-mega grocery store to buy things *I* like to eat—brain food every *kick-ass* fantasy player needs like energy bars, granola bars, candy bars, highly concentrated sugared cereal, Red Bull, Gatorade, ice cream, chewing gum, frozen dinners, dried fruit, popcorn, peanuts, peanut butter and jelly, chips, crackers, string cheese, and beef jerky.

And make sure you have a place to store it. Nothing is more wasteful than building an extension to your home just to stash groceries. Who has time for that, especially my wife? I stack my food along the walls of our bedroom.

Chapter 21

A Lost Art: Executing Uneven Trades That Seem Fair

"Eat and drink with your friends but do not trade with them."
– Turkish Proverb

"B.J. has offered you a trade" is an e-mail alert feared by every league owner. They know, inherently, that by accepting my offer, they probably will lose more than they gain in return. Yet on paper it seems fair. Too damn fair. And that piques their interest. It draws them in. Although history is not on their side, they are sufficiently enticed to accept it on the spot, or at least counter-offer. And a week or two later, once reality has exposed their error in judgment, incomprehensively they want me to proposition them again. Like Lucy repeatedly fooling Charlie Brown with the football, it is completely counterintuitive. It is entirely inconceivable. It is the smooth, seductive dance that I call "executing uneven trades that seem fair."

I am a huge proponent of trading early and often, including during drafts, provided it helps me (and it usually does). As you learned earlier, I once traded up three spots to land the Bears DST, the eventual #1 fantasy scoring DST and sixth highest fantasy scorer *overall* that season. And what did I give up? Three spots in the following round—a sacrifice any *kick-ass* player would make. Never succumb to a "just for the hell of it" trading philosophy. As with all *kick-ass* strategies, trade deliberately and intelligently to ensure that projected benefits outweigh estimated costs.

One note of caution: Don't waste good faith capital trying to wrest someone's #1 player. Unless you offer to trade your #1 player in return, this approach is nothing short of insulting. Any time someone (usually a guy who has never competed against me) proposes sending me two or three decent players for my top guy, I vow never to trade with him again. Overt greed is distasteful in fantasy competition and will earn you silent condemnation (if not worse) from Dirks and Jo-Jos alike.

With that in mind, here are some of my most effective trade strategies:

DRAFT DAY

Top Pick Cutback

You have a very high first round draft pick. After thorough research you have identified a concentration of elite talent, such that dropping a few spots will not adversely impact your pursuit of victory. For example, you might anticipate that, outside of the top four or five RBs, there are also a few QBs and a couple of WRs who legitimately could become the year's #1 fantasy scorer. Or there might be consensus among owners of which players will be picked first and second. If you have one of these two picks, and believe that one or both of these players are overvalued, then trade down in the first round in exchange for trading up in, say, the second and fourth rounds.

What would this mean? You might drop from the second pick to the seventh in the first round and still grab a player you strongly believe will be a top-three scorer. In return you will receive upgrades in the second and fourth rounds, placing you in a significantly better position than your opponents (unbeknownst to them). In a 12-team league this would equate to taking the 18th overall pick (instead of the 23rd), followed by the 26th (your pre-established third round pick), followed by the 42nd (instead of the 47th). Peruse your league's past draft results or the many mock drafts that blanket the Web. Who was selected 18th versus 23rd? How about at 42nd versus 47th? If I am not high on the consensus pick that has fallen into my lap, I would always rather trade down and strengthen my team in the following rounds.

Some competitors are so desperate to snag a top pick that they give up a later round pick altogether. What a coup to trade down on your high first round selection (which you don't want anyway) for an advantageous second round swap and a *free* fourth or fifth rounder. That would grant you five picks in the first four rounds without compromising your draft strategy at the top. This approach works when you tap into your opponents' longing for a supposed fantasy stud whom you know (through superior research) is overrated.

Am I going too fast for you? This is thousand dollar advice, people. Learn it before you get burned by it.

Eye on the Prize

Your pre-draft research has produced three targeted undervalued players at each position. One of them (a QB) has just left the board. Another QB (not on your list) is taken with the next pick. All signs point to a run on this position, and you are still seven picks away from selecting, leaving your two remaining undervalued QBs' impending availability in doubt. It is imperative that you trade up immediately. But don't panic. Simply turn to the guy currently on the clock and state in a clear, calm voice, "Johnny, if you're not sure who to take next, trade it to me with your following pick, and I'll give you my next two picks and my final pick. That way you'll get a boost next round and in the final round."

It is not helpful to call out, "Anyone want to trade?" And quivering, stammering, or fainting will only hurt your cause. While this is a big moment, you must downplay its significance. Even lame fantasy competitors can detect desperation. And don't say ". . . who<u>m</u> to take next . . ."

Grammar counts against you in fantasy draft rooms. Simple words spoken in a friendly, yet firm, manner is the right approach. Also notice I said, ". . . if you're not sure . . ." You are giving Johnny an opening to say "No," which is much less threatening than insisting on a trade, thus making him more open to considering your polite suggestion.

What did I offer? It sounds very reasonable. If Johnny is not sure which player to take, he can pursue a modified *Top Pick Cutback* (a "Middle Pick Cutback") by trading down in a middle round, and then trading up in the next round, followed by a free pick at the end. If he is weighing several selection options, then what does he have to lose? Apparently very little. By trading, he still will land someone useful in this round, followed by a somewhat significant upgrade and then a tiny freebie. Perhaps he will counter-offer. Assuming it is the fifth round of a 12-round draft, he might ask for your ninth rounder instead of a lesser talent from the 12th. If this happens, I still unquestionably accept the deal.

Why? Because now I can claim one of my targeted QBs. Mission accomplished. I have spent hundreds of hours preparing for this draft. I know with great certainty which players are most undervalued and which ones are most likely to finish among the league's leading scorers. If I go into the draft needing at least a QB, two RBs, two WRs, one TE, one K, and one DST, and I have just landed one of my coveted QBs in a middle round without selling the farm (a sixth round downgrade and losing my ninth pick), then I have achieved success. And to those who wonder why I did not draft this QB a round earlier (and thus avoid having to trade players in the later rounds), doing so would have denied me my fourth round pick, whose upside is even higher than the QB's.

By the way, I was poised to utilize this strategy in the 2011 draft mentioned in Chapter 11. After taking one RB and two WRs in the first three rounds, the first of my three coveted QBs was snagged in the middle of the third. Forced to wait another 18 picks before selecting, I braced for the second of my cherished pursuits to leave the board. If that had happened, I would have made an *Eye on the Prize* offer, trading down with my next pick and giving up another in order to secure the last of my undervalued targets. As it turned out, my second option was selected three picks before me, and the next two guys had drafted QBs earlier. So I knew that Matthew Stafford would fall to me in what was one of the draft's biggest steals. And if I had been forced to trade away picks just to land him, it still would have been one of the draft's biggest steals.

Rent-a-Player

Sometimes it is obvious which player an opponent most wants before that player is drafted. It might be a Packers fan who has snatched QB Aaron Rodgers in the first round each of the past three seasons. Or it could be the guy who indiscreetly leaves his cheat-sheet on the table for all to see, with a star or check mark next to a few players with high upsides. Or it could be the newbie who brags about being cousins with a fourth-tier RB. For example, one of my friends vaguely knows former MLB pitcher Darren Dreifort. So during MLB fantasy drafts, the rest of us knew he would pay a little more for a guy he rooted for anyway. Whether obvious or not, your opponents' past and present behavior offers clues into their impending draft decisions. Without compromising your team's future performance, you can capitalize on these insights.

Suppose it is your turn to pick in the opening round, and the Packers fan selects a few spots after you. You might have two or three obvious options at this stage, with Green Bay's QB being one of the best ones. Say to the group, "Can't decide whether to take Rodgers or Calvin Johnson," while glancing at the Packers fan out of the corner of your eye. How does he react? If smart, he will not react at all. Then after about 30 seconds, confidently announce, "I'm taking Rodgers," while again surreptitiously peering his way. What is his reaction now? If he exhibits even a hint of frustration or annoyance, or if he suddenly changes his posture, then you have got him where you want him. Before he makes his first pick, slide over and quietly suggest a "win-win" swap, giving him the QB he covets while improving your draft position in the second and fourth rounds. This might seem like a *Top Pick Cutback* because it is, except instead of unloading a pick, you are handing over a player whose value is greater to someone else.

And even if he does not want to trade right now, you still have a prized QB—and terrific trade bait for the regular season.

REGULAR SEASON

Smackin' a Homer

You can apply the preceding example throughout the regular season to any owner whose devotion to an NFL team or player interferes with common sense, leading him to overpay for talent. I mentioned my friend Eric earlier—the absentee who benefitted from the draft picks I proffered for nothing in return, except defeat. Eric is from just south of Cincinnati (coincidentally, many of my fantasy competitors hail from Ohio). So it was not surprising in 2010 when he drafted the Bengals' #1 RB and #1 WR. I had marked the Bengals' Carson Palmer as an undervalued fourth-tier QB before draft day; while not an every week starter, he certainly was a better option than most prognosticators claimed. I grabbed him late in the draft, and after a few weeks noticed that a free agent QB was posting comparable numbers and possessed even higher long-term upside.

So in exchange for a TE upgrade, I pawned Palmer off to Eric—who was all too willing to pay a premium. Then I promptly reloaded at QB. Palmer finished the season tied for 13th in fantasy points among QBs. He was not going to lead my team to a championship. But he was perfect trade bait to a hometown fan who cared a little too much about the uniform.

Quick Withdrawal

Through your fantasy league's website, propose a trade that is slightly in your favor. That should trigger an e-mail alert to the recipient. Then withdraw it a few seconds later. When clicking on the website to view (or likely reject) your offer, your opponent will discover that you already have. "Why did he cancel it?" he will wonder. Even if he had intended to turn it down, his inner voice will ask, if only momentarily, "Did he think this trade would have helped me?" Then you will have him where you want him.

Two or three days later, call him to discuss trade possibilities. He likely will ask about your rescinded proposal. Tell him you made a mistake, further piquing his interest. After discussing various trade options, say, "Well, it looks like the fairest trade might be the one I withdrew." If he agrees, then you are on your way to a roster upgrade.

Saving the Best for Last

Propose a trade that is clearly yet modestly to your advantage. Do not insult her/his intelligence. Just suggest something that undeniably would benefit you in a small way. After a few minutes, submit a much fairer trade request that still would help you only marginally. On its own, the second offer might seem a bit lopsided. But when judged next to your earlier offer, it will appear much more palatable to your opponent.

Woeful Makeover

One or more of your competitors will begin the season horribly. Faced with a 1-3 or 0-4 record, he might want to shake things up. That is when you enter. Desperate owners trade out of desperation, which handicaps them at the outset of negotiations. He might have a top-flight QB who is underperforming due to a difficult early season schedule. However, he does not rationalize it in this way. Instead your opponent laments how "tired" he is of his QB, and how he needs to "revamp" his roster. You will not receive many better trade opportunities that year. So circle late September on your calendar and get ready to pounce.

Gaming the Competition

Float some of your underperforming stars as trade bait to fellow owners, suggesting (not "offering") deals that *would* have seemed fair when the season started. For example, casually establish whether a guy is willing to exchange his hot-starting, second-tier WR for your underperforming, first-tier WR. If he says, "Go to hell," then wait for the mediocre WR's surprising play to level off and for your fantasy stud to rebound to top-tier status. Then do a *Quick Withdrawal*, subtly reminding him what he could have had. Such gamesmanship keeps opponents off balance, regretting not trading when they had the chance. Profit off of their remorse, as they will be more likely to consider your next *real* trade request for a player that you really want.

Bye-Bye

Suppose you are scheduled to play against Jake in Week 9. A few weeks earlier, offer him a player who will be on a bye in Week 9. This approach works only when your research shows that either the player is overvalued, or a suitable replacement is readily available (either via this trade or free agency). This strategy is most effective when the bye is far enough in the future that your opponent fails to make the connection.

If your team is 6-0 and looking strong for the playoffs, then this trade is not as necessary. But if you are 4-2 and seeking an edge against a team that you must beat later to bolster your playoff hopes, then have fun exploiting the NFL schedule. And make sure whomever you receive in return has taken his bye. Otherwise you have wasted the opportunity, and I will laugh at you.

If your prey does not bite, then make a comparable offer to each owner. For example, if it is Week 6 and three of your players have byes in weeks 9 and 10, then consider trading one or packaging two in a single offer. Before choosing which future on-bye players to shop, analyze who has the toughest schedule going forward. Which teams are more likely to rest their starters during critical fantasy weeks 16 and 17? And so on. Even if the players you receive in return are of equal value to those you gave away, as long as they took their bye earlier, this seemingly fair trade benefits you.

Hit Him While He's Hurt

This strategy is useful in leagues where teams have few bench spots. Lacking sufficient reserve space to house his injured and on-bye players, Frank must start two inactive players one week. His injured players suffer from week-to-week ailments, meaning his team could return full strength in the next week or two. Meanwhile, there are no free agent upgrades available. Frank is screwed. And it is your job to save him—at least for one week—while improving your roster for the long term.

Thanks to planning ahead, you have plenty of bench space to add a player who is on a bye. Offer Frank a decent replacement—someone better than any waiver option, but not quite better than the bye player he is forced to start, and which you justifiably have targeted. If desperately needing a win that week, Frank will be more prone to taking your player and the short-term gain. In return you will gain a positional upgrade for future games, including the playoffs.

I executed this approach perfectly early in my 2011-2012 NBA fantasy league after an opponent lost a center to a long-term injury. The weekly add/drop period had just passed, leaving him with absolutely no lineup replacement. His poor planning and bad luck became my reward. But rather than propose an overtly lopsided exchange with questionable probability of success, I offered a serviceable center (drafted in the 15th round of our 14-team league) and a guard (my seventh rounder / 87th player taken overall) for one of his forwards (a sixth rounder / 72nd player taken overall). It was a win-win, in that we both got what we wanted.

But my win happened to be a little bigger.

*   *   *

This last anecdote highlights a critically important lesson for any aspiring *kick-ass* fantasy manager: Be outwardly respectful toward your opponents. While their trade offers might piss you off, be the bigger person; send polite e-mails explaining that it is not the right swap at this time, but that you are open to other possibilities in the future. Develop a reputation for being approachable so that when opponents are in the trading mood, they will think of you first—not because you are a pushover, but because you exude kindness and fairness. Congratulate them on a great start to the season, or wish them well in an upcoming matchup against a mutual nemesis. Naturally, they have no idea how much of a Dirk Hardy you really are. And that is part of Dirk's mystique: Be the best, but don't strut around like you know it.

This attitude will increase your likelihood of bettering your squad through player swaps. I have observed competitors shunning any and all trade options for *years*, driving them dangerously close to Jo-Jo Land. As a *kick-ass* manager, you make it your business to know more about each player—your own, your opponents', and free agents—than anyone else. Your peerless expertise makes opponents look like idiots while making them *think* they look like champions. Such overconfidence drives my competitors to click "Accept" even after they have been burned by past trades; they still think, "This time I'm getting the better end of the deal."

But as long as you continue working harder than they are, they will almost always grab the short end of the fantasy stick.

CHAPTER 22

THOSE UNRELIABLE GUT FEELINGS

"The value given to the testimony of any feeling
must depend on our whole philosophy, not our whole philosophy on a feeling."
– C.S. Lewis

As the season progresses, many people abandon previously successful strategies. Whether due to laziness, arrogance, boredom, or amnesia, they begin relying instead on those dreaded "gut feelings."

Back when I ran an almost award-winning *kick-ass* fantasy football blog, a reader posted a comment asking whether I would incorporate *gut feelings* into my unparalleled prognostications. This misguided soul was under the crazy impression that our guts hold valuable insights into which underrated QB will toss three or more TDs next week, or which lower-tier TE will finish among the top 10 in positional scoring.

Neither hunches nor senses nor impulses make champions. If they are natural outcomes of empirical and quantifiable evidence gathered and scrutinized objectively, then sure, have fun with instincts that simply mirror what you know. But like our friend Jo-Jo Mc'scuses, too many fantasy owners believe leagues can be won by taking shortcuts, forgoing deliberate research and analysis in favor of listening to that which has no voice: *gut feelings.*

> ***Me:*** *"Jo-Jo, how does your team look this week?"*
>
> ***Jo-Jo:*** *"I'm feeling really good about it."*

Me: *"Why?"*

Jo-Jo: *"It's . . . it's kinda hard to say."*

Me: *"Try. For me."*

Jo-Jo: *"Well, I've got this quarterback who's looked shaky the past few games. So I'm pretty sure he's gonna turn things around."* [He wipes his nose with the back of a snot-stained hand.] *"Then there's the trade I just made to get this running back. He scored 20 fantasy points last week."*

Me: *"So he's a perennial fantasy stud?"*

Jo-Jo: *"He actually started pretty slowly. But after six or seven weeks, he finally proved himself last Sunday. He looks really tough. I think it's a sign of things to come."*

While some of you might pity Jo-Jo, let's not lose sleep over him. He has no demonstrable understanding of his team's anticipated performance. He is "pretty sure" his underperforming QB will have a better game this time. Why? Is he facing a bad or injury-depleted defense? Did the QB or one of his coaches recently disclose that they are working hard to kick-start the passing game? Has the QB been ill or mentally unprepared previously, whereas now he is 100% ready to thrive? If he is a premier talent at his position, then the *rebound effect* would indicate an eventual return to greatness—but not if his slump is due to persisting issues.

And what about his fearsome RB? Judge players by how they play, not by how they appear. Factoring unquantifiable variables such as weather, player motivation, and coaching strategy are perfectly acceptable. Factoring facial expressions are pointless. And why did this RB suddenly perform well last week after several relatively disappointing games? As with our earlier Chris Brown example, unless Jo-Jo has researched this player thoroughly, he has no clue whether this recent roster addition will continue making sizable contributions on the fantasy scoreboard.

Gut feelings are excuses for mental lethargy. They are stale residue from so many weeks and years ago—entirely unreliable opinions based on what we once knew, rather than on what we should know right now. Too many Jo-Jos seek the easy way out. If faring well, no longer as motivated to further improve their team, they kick back and relax and wait for the wins to keep mounting. If faring poorly, they almost blindly add players with great recent performances and hope for the best, never conceiving that a player with lesser stats might possess far greater short- and long-term fantasy potential.

Kick-ass managers, on the other hand, take smart risks when evidence demonstrates a high probability of success. Instincts alone cannot lead you to victory. At best they are distractions—at worst, agents of futility. Remove them from your fantasy equation entirely. The *kick-ass* player examines matchups, reads news reports, updates one's player matrix, and weighs statistical probabilities, leading to implementable strategies that meet both short-term goals (winning the upcoming week's matchup) and long-term goals (winning the championship).

Let's examine a real-world example: In 2007 the Raiders' starting RB, Dominic Rhodes, was suspended for the season's first four games. By now you should know that suspensions, holdouts, injuries, and the like—unless impacting one your high-performing players—are fantasy gold. While slow-footed opponents reel from the loss, you swoop in to snatch any backup with higher fantasy scoring potential than at least one of your existing players. So imagine my joy when reading that LaMont Jordan would assume full-time RB duties until Rhodes' return.

My gut might have warned me that no players—particularly interim starters—are guaranteed to thrive in such a short-term capacity. Hell, they might even lose the job to a third-stringer before the end of the first contest. But as always, my gut was overruled by truth. I read the local news, reviewed all relevant stats, and recognized Jordan's desire to capitalize on this four-game opportunity, which came at the tail end of his prime playing years. A former NFL starter, he was less likely than most promoted players to fold under the pressure. He was two years removed from a 1,025-rushing-yard (3.8 yards per carry), 563-receiving-yard, nine-TD campaign. He suffered a season-ending injury with Oakland the following year, while Rhodes started all 16 games for the powerhouse Colts and finished with a relatively paltry 641 rushing yards (3.4 yards per carry), 251 receiving yards, and five TDs.

When all signs point to starting a player, start him. If you are worried about others thinking you are nuts, then you are no better than Jo-Jo, caring more about competitors' pure conjecture than your hard-earned, rational conclusions. "But it's too risky starting a 28-year-old journeyman with only one great season under his belt." If your gut has the final say in roster matters regardless of objective facts, then you deserve to lose. "Let's wait and see how he does the first week before putting him in the lineup." Stop being a wuss. That summer the Raiders had selected QB JaMarcus Russell as the draft's first overall pick. I knew that head coaches often engineered a more conservative, run-heavy offense when starting rookie

QBs—especially in their first NFL game. Additionally, their Week 1 opponent was the Lions, who had netted the fifth fewest DST points the previous season while coughing up 125 rushing yards per contest.

My commitment to *kick-ass* research and reasoning prevailed, as should yours. I picked up Jordan, moved him into my starting lineup, and posted on my blog that he would be that week's #1 undervalued RB performer.

The result? Jordan finished the game with 70 rushing yards, 89 receiving yards, and a TD, earning a tie for the league's most RB fantasy points that week. And this undrafted, generally unheralded player did not slow down, averaging 118 rushing yards during the following three games and scoring in Week 3, outperforming nearly every other RB in the first four games of 2007.

At this point my initial gut feeling was, "This guy is your meal ticket to the title." But for any Dirk Hardy, such groundless judgments are worthless in the face of diligent investigation. A Jo-Jo would have continued starting Jordan for the foreseeable future, at least until his stellar play subsided. But a Dirk knows when to cut bait (see Chapter 17). A Dirk does not care how others perceive him. He knows what he is doing and why he is doing it. The goal is winning, whatever it takes, however unpopular or strange the decisions might seem.

And so with the Raiders facing a Week 5 bye and Dominic Rhodes returning from suspension, I dumped my star RB. My opponents thought I was crazy. Yet they failed to see the stack of evidence showing that Rhodes would make enough of an impact to slow Jordan's momentum. As a result, multiple free agent RBs held more short- and long-term value than Jordan did. Your gut might try to trick you into following supposed "common sense," when in fact only your brain knows the answers. Retain your players—even your best players—*only* if their anticipated rate of return cannot be matched by free agents.

You might be wondering what happened to my four-week savior. He started the next three games over Rhodes, finishing with 18, 11, and 12 carries, respectively, and averaging only 29 rushing yards, 28 receiving yards, and zero TDs per contest. Over the final nine games, Jordan had only 38 rushing yards, 33 receiving, and one TD. Per game? No, total. With Rhodes back in the mix and young RB Justin Fargas receiving more opportunities, the Raiders no longer made room for their early season hero.

Jordan was like a solid investment that for a few weeks damn near turned the stock market on its head. But you must learn when to enjoy the ride and when to get out; your future as an investor in great fantasy players depends on it. I took a lot of ribbing after Week 4 for dropping one of the top fantasy performers of the young season. But when comparing facts to perception, facts win every time.

A gut feeling will never grant you a higher probability of success than conclusions cultivated through comprehensive research and high-level fantasological thinking. If you want to take the easy way out, compose your weekly lineup by following your fickle heart. If you want to take the *kick-ass* way in, shut up and do your homework.

Chapter 23

Offsetting the Inconvenience
of Obligatory Travel

"But you can travel on for ten thousand miles, and still stay where you are."
– Harry Chapin

Try as one might, no one is immune from the perils of travel. I am not speaking of high-speed police chases, being stuck on an airport runway for eight hours, or checking into a hotel so infested with mice that three work as porters. Rather, I am referring to how travel threatens one's very fantasy existence.

Simply put, if you have complete control over when and where to travel, don't go. In fact, between the fantasy draft and championship week, avoid leaving your house. Winning requires total focus on winning, period. But if travel is rigidly thrust upon you in an unseemly manner, here are a few tips to mitigate fantasy fallout.

At First, Just Say "No"

Even if your spouse forces you—under threat of no nookie for a decade—to visit your in-laws for Thanksgiving, initially tell her "No." "No" does not mean you will not go (see aforementioned abstinence threat), but rather draws a faint line in the sand as you welcome further discussion. Soon you and your partner will reach a satisfactory compromise, whereby you agree to join her and the kids, but will be free to do pre- and postgame research and watch all three Thursday games. Plus you will return home early Sunday morning, thus preserving your critical game viewing routine.

If you had not put your foot down initially, you would have been stuck with a long weekend of TV-free meals, G-rated movie outings, and charades. Lots and lots of charades.

Don't Drive

Your company is short-listed for a huge government contract. The interview is tomorrow morning, 100 miles away. Depending on traffic and departure time, you anticipate roughly a two-hour drive with minimal fantasy research opportunities—in other words, two hours wasted behind the wheel. Sure, you could scan satellite radio stations from every NFL city, hoping to hear something useful. But the odds are against learning anything earth-shattering from a radio program, especially since you intend to scour the Internet right before you get in the car.

So remember this lesson: never drive anywhere. It is one of the most fantasologically inefficient modes of travel ever invented. You are left with three reasonable alternatives:

(1) *Take a taxi.* This option takes about as much time as driving yourself, except you have full Internet capabilities (assuming access to a mobile device, which you should have bought before the season started). The only downside is if your driver talks incessantly about anything other than the latest fantasy football news.

(2) *Fly.* Assuming a 30-minute taxi ride to the airport, arriving one hour early, a 45-minute flight, 10 minutes to de-plane, and a 30-minute taxi ride to the interview site, you are investing almost one extra hour flying versus traveling by car, but with less risk of getting stuck in traffic jams. You also have Internet access nearly the whole time (particularly with today's continually expanding

in-flight Internet options), as well as a comfortable seat, drinks, and a functional tray table.

(3) *Persuade a co-worker to drive you.* If your employer is unwilling to pay for a taxi or plane, then convince a co-worker to drive you to and from the interview. If there are no takers, grab an intern or a low-level staffer itching for a résumé builder like "Assisted with interview preparation for multimillion dollar government contract."

Ask for Help

Desperate co-workers are not the only people capable of aiding your fantasy operations. Family members are most valuable when supporting you during obligatory trips. Enlist your kids to call sports reporters requesting insights into "my favorite players in the whole wide world." Tap your significant other to crunch numbers and assess which free agent DSTs have the easiest fantasy playoff matchups. Solicit your retired father living in Chicago to visit Soldier Field to assess how your top-tier RB with a "questionable" injury tag looks during pregame warm-ups. While you endure an all-day business trip, your family has logged a combined 30 hours in *kick-ass* fantasy research. Way to go, team!

Reap Time Zone Benefits

Several years ago my ESPN league's drop/add system locked immediately upon the week's first kickoff and then unlocked every Tuesday at 3:30 a.m. EST. In other words, the hottest free agent pickups stemming from the most recent performances / injuries / depth chart shifts were available to anyone dedicated enough to wake up at 3:30 a.m. I was not yet a fully functional *kick-ass* manager, so sleep was still preferable to winning at all costs (I cringe when recalling my youthful indiscretions). Nevertheless one of my two co-managers had planned a trip to Ireland with his wife during the season's first two weeks.

This seemingly distracting, anti-fantasy venture turned out to be a boon for our team. At that time of year, Ireland was four hours ahead of the East Coast of the United States. So 3:30 a.m. our time was 7:30 a.m. in Ireland. Long before any other league managers awoke, my friend simply rolled out of bed a few minutes before 7:30 a.m. (Ireland time), dropped our team's worst players, and added the most valuable free agents.

This was the same season we started 9-0, and it was no coincidence. With this ideal waiver system in place, our co-manager's time zone shift was a difference maker.

He never should have returned.

Upgrade

If you fly, upgrade to first class, and as highlighted earlier in this chapter, procure Web access. If you stay in a hotel, secure the highest available Internet speed. If your commitment is overseas, purchase a VPN blocker to ensure continual coverage of NFL programming not necessarily available outside the U.S. Fantasy victory and cutting corners don't mix. Identify and benefit from all available resources to guarantee, at a minimum, technological parity with your opponents.

*   *   *

I am writing this entire book from Mumbai, India. No joke. Work commitments moved my family around the planet for a two-year stint in the world's most populated city. At this moment, a shirtless man is brushing his teeth on the rooftop next door. Again, no joke.

During Daylight Savings Time, about 90% of NFL games are played between 10:30 p.m. and 4:30 a.m. India time. After DST ends in October, these games run between 11:30 p.m. and 5:30 a.m. Internet access is less reliable here than in the States. It is not uncommon for the power to go out for long stretches. Needless to say, it is a challenging place to be a *kick-ass* manager.

But when your job sends you overseas, take stock of both positive and negative impacts to fantasy success. The key is minimizing each downside while accentuating built-in advantages. One positive is the element of surprise: Don't tell anyone in your league about your impending move. Like my friend who visited Ireland, you might have an edge over competitors in acquiring free agents from a different time zone. If other league owners catch wind of your life change before the season begins, they likely will change the rules to level the playing field.

In fact, go one step further and propose rule changes that will benefit you in your new surroundings. If your new time zone means you will be awake while your opponents sleep, the best drop/add strategy is one where free agency is "open to everyone" beginning in the middle of the night in whatever time zone your opponents are competing. As a result, you will get prime pickings each week, leaving the scraps to everyone else.

What you *don't* want is a drop/add system that permits free agent pickups around the clock. Under this arrangement, your opponents could add hot prospects off the wire at any time—including while you are sleeping. If a team announces on Wednesday at 4:00 p.m. EST (Thursday at 2:30 a.m. your time, for example) that RB B is the new starter, relegating the underperforming RB A to about 10 carries per game, who is primed to grab free agent RB B? Certainly not you, nestled in your bed with the covers pulled up tight. Multiply that scenario by 100, and you can see how waiver rules could make or break the season of anyone living at least a few time zones away from fellow league members.

Politicians view the world through ideology and one-upmanship. Architects view the world through the built environment. Fantasologists like you and me view the world as the assemblage of rules, players, and numbers that form statistical probabilities of future results. Regardless of travel commitments, when we harness the power of rules, players, and numbers in our favor, we cannot lose.

But it's always easier at home on your couch.

PART IV

THE POSTSEASON

Famous Days in Fantasy Football History

November 4, 1984

The Seattle Seahawks' defense scores four touchdowns—
all on interception returns—for high school teacher Billy
Matthews' **Go-Go-Ghostbusters**.

That would have been enough to defeat attorney Rosetta
Fandango's **Mary Lou Retton Vaulters** and overtake her
for the last playoff spot. However, he loses by three
points, as the league commissioner's broken answering
machine fails to record Mr. Matthews' pregame request to
activate the Seahawks from his bench.

CHAPTER 24

STEP IT UP

"For with slight efforts how should we obtain great results?
It is foolish even to desire it."
– Euripides

A word to the not yet wise: Clinching a spot in your league playoffs does not make you a fantasy mastermind. The world is overrun with those who have achieved near greatness. Will your life continue to be the sum of regular season letdowns sprinkled with playoff defeats? Perhaps earning a tombstone-worthy epitaph commemorating a life truly wasted?

Here Lies
[Your Name]
- Fantasy Sports Competitions: **78**
- Playoff Appearances: **25**
- Championships: **4**

(I am giving you the benefit of the doubt regarding the four championships.)

Or will you become something far more impressive—a brilliant and motivated creature who future generations will remember fondly?

Here Lies
[Your Name]
"Fantasologist"
- Fantasy Sports Competitions: **78**
- Playoff Appearances: **74**
- Championships: **65**

Your existence holds more promise than you might realize, and also includes potential pitfalls based on that most vulgar fantasy sin: premature pride. Postseason appearances alone are meaningless. So stop viewing the playoffs as a milestone. They deserve no such credit, no such honor. Who cares if you dominate most regular seasons if such supposed supremacy rarely generates titles? Ask the 1968-'69 Colts if they consider themselves that season's best team, as the Jets merely were AFL lightweights who got lucky. Or ask the seemingly superlative 2001-'02 Rams if they enjoyed a successful campaign, despite enduring a Super Bowl upset at the hands of the upstart Patriots. Or ask the 2007-'08 Patriots if their undefeated season (minus just one final game) made them pseudo champions in spirit.

Getting carried away by regular season accolades often leads one to failure. Postseason berths should be cause to work harder, longer, and smarter. Whether improbable or anticipated, clinching a fantasy playoff spot is not a reset button, but a ramp-up button. Do not adjust strategies. Do not question logic. Your *kick-ass* approach brought you here; now exploit your greatest weapon like never before.

Conduct a top-to-bottom examination of your player matrix, pinpointing potential acquisition targets meriting future study. Assuming the trade deadline has passed, you can disregard other teams' rosters. Instead focus on your own players and the 150-200 free agents who possess at least a slim probability of improving your team during any of the coming weeks. Learn *everything* about each of these athletes and their teams, eliminating from consideration any player with less probability of fantasy success than your rostered players at the same position.

At this point in the NFL season, some athletes come out of nowhere to shine, whether because of injuries or a team's commitment to start different players—either to rest their stars for the NFL playoffs, or to get a jump on evaluating talent for next season. Get inside the minds of coaching staffs; what new personnel strategies will they implement? Get inside the heads of unproven talent who possess the skills, determination, and opportunities to make names for themselves in the year's final contests.

Honor your season by exhibiting good judgment when it matters most. Maximize your return on all empirical analysis. Which players face a "perfect storm" of statistical advantages? Which players face challenging elements that call into question their true value? I have witnessed countless fantasy studs fall flat during these closing weeks, crippling seemingly unstoppable fantasy teams' title hopes. Many such letdowns were predictable based on numerous factors including defensive matchups, splitting time with backup players, coaches' inclinations to rest star players, and so on. Show no allegiance toward great players who, based on your sound predictions, deserve to be benched.

Scout your opponent's weaknesses. Depending on bench size, wreak maximum havoc on his pickup/drop strategy, blocking his anticipated moves by grabbing free agents he most covets. In addition, isolate future opponents' weaknesses. Who might you face in the next round, and what is his most pressing need?

These strategies should look familiar, as they are among many you have learned throughout these chapters. Leave nothing on the table, nothing to chance. Quantify the positive impact of every possible roster, as well as the scoring potential of every possible lineup. There are no shortcuts. There are no reprieves.

By choosing to read this book, you have pledged to transcend mediocrity. Now is the time to embrace this challenge head-on. Your family can wait. Your boss can wait. Your dog can wait. But never leave a championship waiting.

CHAPTER 25

CONCESSION SPEECH: JO-JO MC'SCUSES

"Only the wisest and stupidest of men never change."
– Confucius

Jo-Jo is making his way to the podium. Let's listen:

"Today . . . I consider myself . . . the unluckiest person in fantasy football. Yet another season of just barely missing the playoffs. I should have won the championship. My team was that good. But an array of injuries and bafflingly poor performances were too damaging to overcome.

"My season started so promising. I drafted several players that my fantasy magazine predicted would be great. I won my first two games without too much trouble. Then the fantasy gods began laying their path of destruction.

"First my #2 WR tore his ACL and was lost for the year. Then my #1 TE moved into a time-share with his backup, absolutely destroying his production.

"After Week 6 I planned to pick up a stud rookie who came out of nowhere to become a

top 10 RB. But my stupid boss called me into a meeting; by the time I got out, my lame roommate had claimed the RB. He should have been mine. Stupid work.

"Then I met this woman who was really cool, and she insisted we go ice skating on Sunday. Since I don't meet women very often, I said yes. So I was out Sunday morning of Week 9 when it was announced that my starting QB was a last-minute scratch with bruised ribs. Of all the bad luck . . .

"Oh yeah, and there was the time in Week 11 when my #1 WR had a touchdown called back because of some phantom penalty. Even the announcers knew it was a dumb call. That score would have given me nine more points. Instead I lost that week by four.

"Bad luck seems to follow me every season. But as long as I keep doing what I'm doing, the breaks will start going my way."

Jo-Jo Mc'scuses wraps up a 6-7 season the only way he knows how: complaining. He distributes blame like Halloween candy. He is a sore loser with no desire to understand why he lost.

As you now know, *kick-ass* managers earn championships through hard work and intelligence. It matters little how many of your players get hurt, demoted, or suspended. It is largely irrelevant whether your star QB has an off year. Shit happens. When it hits us in the face, we wipe it off and keep moving forward. When it hits Jo-Jo, he takes a picture of it as proof of his misfortune.

The only way you will become a consistent fantasy football champion is by adopting Dirk-like sensibilities in your daily life. Jo-Jo has nothing to offer you, because clearly he has nothing to offer himself.

CHAPTER 26

VICTORY SPEECH: DIRK HARDY

"First they ignore you, then they laugh at you, then they fight you, then you win."
– Mahatma Gandhi

You may have noticed that Dirk has not contributed many words to this book. That is because he has been too busy focusing on a more pressing matter: winning the championship. He leads not with words, but by example. With prize money in hand, he will honor us now with his thoughts:

"It was another tough season. Perfection was always the goal, but never the expectation. I sought only to dominate through superior planning and execution. Once again, my efforts paid off.

"Losing is never easy. Defeat kicked me in the ass three times this season: weeks 2, 5, and 10. For those contests I prepared just as hard and for just as long as in other weeks. I worked hard to learn from these losses, highlighting weaknesses in my team and prompting me to make adjustments.

"Similarly, I learned from each of my wins. After all, victories are not conclusions; they are stepping stones along a path to greatness. Before taking each next step, I repositioned my seemingly invincible squad, transforming it into an even more unbeatable team for my next matchup.

"Obviously, a high probability of success does not guarantee success. I am not perfect because I cannot predict the future. Through diligent research and analysis, I can assign only probabilities for future events. When measured against this realistic ideal, I fared pretty well.

"I would like to thank my family and friends for being supportive from afar. And I would like to thank my competitors, who once again were not as committed to victory as I was."

To fully appreciate Dirk's brilliance, let's examine a couple of obstacles he overcame to reach this point. His first round draft pick—the #1 projected QB ("QB A") in the league—went down with a season-ending injury in Week 2. After a comprehensive online analysis and several phone calls to sports writers, Dirk released the QB and his #4 WR, picked up that QB's backup ("QB B"), and added the upcoming week's projected #1 available QB ("QB C")—a guy facing a very weak pass rush and pass defense. He covered two angles in the process, ensuring a competitive option in Week 3 (QB C) while also securing a potentially valuable long-term replacement (QB B).

Dirk continually reassessed his QB situation throughout the season. "Who has the highest probability of scoring the most fantasy points in his next game? And in the game after that?" He ran through eight QBs in 15 weeks, never starting one more than two contests in a row—not due to gut feelings or superstition, but because a better QB matchup existed elsewhere. As a result, his QBs collectively averaged just over 21 points per game, which was the third highest average in the league at that position. Dirk would have preferred to ride his star QB straight to the title. But life does not always work out that way. Instead he developed a foolproof, *kick-ass* backup plan. If QB B excelled, terrific. If QB B never came close to matching QB A's numbers, then Dirk felt confident continuing to cycle through QBs C, D, and whoever else was the best free agent QB in a given week. And because of Dirk's unrivaled research and analysis, his predictions usually were accurate.

Most drafts' first rounds include at least a couple of busts: players who significantly underperform or get hurt early/often. In 2008 many Jo-Jos effectively lost the championship in the first quarter of Week 1, when their #1 pick—QB Tom Brady—was knocked out for the season with a severe left knee injury. This fantasy heavyweight had scored the most fantasy points *overall* in 2007; in fact, he had 33% more points than the #2 league scorer, teammate WR Randy Moss. Few fantasy players have been so highly touted entering a season. Anyone lucky enough to win the 2008 #1 overall pick was presumed to be the early favorite for the title.

But in a flash, Jo-Jos around the world cried out in bitter agony. "Why me!!!???" Not Dirk, who proved above how to compensate for such a setback. *Kick-ass* managers in 2008 understood this, too. Brady's replacement, Matt Cassel, came out of nowhere to finish the season ranked 14th among fantasy scorers across all positions. On five occasions—often predictably—he threw for three or more TDs. In two of those games he tallied 400+ passing yards. Four of his five big days came in weeks 11, 12, 15, and 16, helping his owners reach the playoffs and then dominate their postseason contests. When combined with the output of selectively activated "mediocre" QBs with terrific matchups and other favorable conditions, *kick-ass* owners received all of the QB production they needed to win. Losing Brady sucked. But it did not suck the life out of smart fantasy managers' championship hopes.

Dirk's fourth round draft pick, a second-tier WR ("WR B"), also dealt our hero a blow when the normally reliable 32-year-old started losing targets to a rising rookie WR ("WR A") in Week 5. Until that game, WR B was averaging nine targets per contest and was on pace for 83 receptions, 1,114 receiving yards, and eight TDs. But in his fifth game, WR B was targeted only four times, catching four balls for 42 yards and a score.

On paper this was a solid outing—enough fantasy points from a second-tier WR to keep owners like Jo-Jo from worrying too much. But Dirk saw the big picture. WR B's team's QB might be developing a better rapport with WR A, who logged eight targets, seven receptions, and 83 yards in Week 5 after being nearly invisible during the season's first four games. Was this a temporary blip, as with so many mediocre players who break out a few times per year? Or was this the start of a long-term trend?

Since Dirk did not know the answer, he studied the hell out of WR A, WR B, their QB, and the coaching staff right after the Week 5 contest ended. He found evidence that the team wanted to groom WR A into a #1 receiver—if not this year, then next year. There also was talk that, since WR B's contract was expiring at the end of this season, and with the team 0-5, the team wanted to give more opportunities to younger talent.

Dirk determined that WR A would be a better long-term option than WR B. To test his theory, he released a reserve fourth-tier WR and added WR A. Week 6's output—

a repeat of Week 5's surprising receiver disparity—reinforced that Dirk had learned something significant before any other league owner caught on. By Week 8, WR A was entrenched as his team's #1 receiving threat, while WR B was relegated to four to five targets for 50-60 yards per game.

This "changing of the guard" occurs throughout every NFL season at multiple positions and throughout the depth charts. For example, after catching 60 balls for 944 yards and nine TDs in 2010, WR Mario Manningham was the Giants' clear-cut #2 WR entering the following season. CBSSports projected him as a top 20 WR fantasy scorer. But a combination of injuries (he played in only 11 games) and the rise of the relatively unknown WR Victor Cruz (who competed for a roster spot in the preseason and wound up with the second most fantasy points among all WRs) made Manningham nearly irrelevant. Those who identified this depth chart shift early reaped the rewards; those who did not lost out.

Through superior effort and application, Dirk turned bad luck into good and sometimes great production. That is why he won. It was not only because he drafted the best team, and he certainly was not the luckiest. Quite simply, he earned it through hard work and paying attention. He secured an optimal number of top-tier talent at the draft, made the most of his mediocre talent throughout the season, and acquired free agents that became solid replacements for his injured/demoted stars.

Dirk wins because he wants to—because he is willing to do whatever it takes. If you share this singularly focused determination, then you will win, too. Every year.

PART V

THE OFFSEASON (REDUX)

Famous Days in Fantasy Football History

December 12, 1976

With a roster that includes seven of the league's top 10 fantasy scorers, twins Jake and Joanne McGuirk face Stanley Ludwig's **Disco Ducks** for the championship. With confidence to spare, the McGuirks add New England Patriots receiver and childhood friend Steve Burks to their starting lineup.

In this, the year's final regular season game, Burks doubles his season reception total, finishing the game with 17 yards on one catch and helping to lift the McGuirks' **Bostontennials** to an 80-point victory.

CHAPTER 27

VICTORY BANQUET

"Everybody, sooner or later, sits down to a banquet of consequences."
– Robert Louis Stevenson

The Parable of the Fantasy Victory Banquet

There once was a fantasy football champion who prepared a victory banquet. He sent postal carriers to his league opponents inviting them to the banquet, but the opponents refused to come.

Then he sent some more postal carriers and said, "Tell those who have been invited that I have prepared them dinner: orange soda and Hot Pockets have been procured, and everything is ready. Come to the victory banquet."

But they paid no attention and went off—one to his business, another to his son's middle school basketball game, and another to join his wife in the bedroom.

Then the champion said to the postal carriers, "The victory banquet is ready, but those I invited did not come. Go to their homes and places of work and re-invite them." So despite this being outside their job description, the postal carriers went out to gather the league opponents, and the champion's combination living-dining room soon was filled with his guests.

But when the champion came in to see the guests, he noticed a man there who was not a member of his league. "Friend," he asked, "how did you get in here if you are not an opponent?" The man was speechless.

Then the champion told the postal carriers (who were waiting in line for orange soda), "Tie him hand and foot, and throw him outside into the darkness. For many are invited, but few are chosen."

I love a good victory banquet. It is my way of telling opponents, "Thank you for being in my life." Their Jo-Jo-like tendencies on the fantasy battlefield make my championship goals that much easier to attain.

So while sharing a meal with vanquished foes is a time to honor your success, it also is a time to celebrate others' participation in the great American pastime of fantasy sports. When holding your banquet, make certain your fellow league members appreciate the honor of being invited to such a special event. The coming together of friends / colleagues / worthy acquaintances for a semi-formal and festive gathering is what separates us from the apes, who frankly don't understand anything about fantasy football, and who sadly don't even care to. "Few are chosen." How true. Among Earth's millions of species, only one has the capacity to draft, adjust rosters, set lineups, and spend prize money. Urge your guests to ruminate on this.

Also honor your opponents individually, singling out anecdotes concerning superior decision making and fair play.

Some hosts elect to distribute awards; others prefer a more casual affair. Regardless of your personal style, be magnanimous in victory. Celebrate others' achievements. Make them feel grateful for competing in a league where their exploits—however futile in the end—are recognized.

Your graciousness surely will pay dividends down the road, as your defeated competitors will like you more for displaying such generosity. For example, you have begun to identify which rule changes would benefit your style of play. Inspiring intra-league loyalty will make it easier to enact these modifications. Which draft style works best for you? Which waiver system plays into your time zone and your *kick-ass* approach? Do you have more bench spots than you will ever need? Or not enough? When you next propose rule changes, league members who like you will be more open to considering your recommendations. Furthermore, during the season these members are more likely to ponder trade proposals from people they respect than from those they don't.

Finally, after everyone has been amply nourished and entertained, convert your victory banquet into a football viewing party. While the Super Bowl is optimal, the AFC/NFC championship is a suitable substitute. Bond with league members over great plays, hard hits, and fitting commentary. All of you are now on the same team—the team known as *Football Fans*. And no fantasy contest, no matter how competitive and bitter, can tear this team apart.

A successful banquet is the Band-Aid that heals all wounds. And rest assured, there will be plenty of time to inflict new fantasy wounds next season.

CHAPTER 28

WAS IT WORTH IT?

"When you can whip any man in the world, you never know peace."
– Muhammad Ali

Throughout these pages I have divulged age-old secrets and innovative concepts to challenge your way of thinking. From choosing the right league to avoiding an awful team name, you are now an expert. From dominating your draft to engineering favorable trade outcomes, you are uniquely equipped. From knowing when to add a player to understanding when to cut one loose, you are truly gifted. And no one can take this away from you.

However, fantasy football is not a static enterprise to be mastered and then left on the dining room table with your stack of Bosley Medical hair restoration bills. For what good is mastery if it does not serve as a gateway for *further* mastery? Your path to success does not end here. I have given you the tools to begin applying your newfound expertise. To thrive year after year, you must continually build upon it.

Upon first cracking open this book, you were but an infant, still unable to walk. In fact, the concept of *walking* seemed foreign to you. "How could anyone truly walk, or even want to walk, when crawling is a perfectly acceptable mode of transportation?" Then you began to read. With each succeeding chapter your perspective grew while your range of thought expanded. Soon you started to walk, at first slowly and hesitantly, and then faster and more sure-footedly.

Then you learned a new kind of step—one that kept both feet airborne simultaneously, albeit for very brief yet repetitive spurts. Yes, you were now running, navigating through and over and around obstacles in your path. Faster and faster, with increasing stamina, you developed efficient form and unwavering resolve, catapulting over the longest distances and to the greatest heights imaginable. You could achieve any feat simply by putting your mind to it, and then trusting in your physical abilities to follow through.

But what happens to runners who stop running, who forsake exercise for sloth, sleep, and Funyuns? Their sterling physical form erodes, leaving mush and couch stains in their wake. Their greatness is measured in memories, not in realized potential. They have become, in essence, "what might have been."

So was this literary journey worth it? It depends on your next move. Will you apply my strategies during next season's first few weeks, then decide they are too hard and/or time-consuming? Will one fantasy decision go awry, leading to a complete and utterly moronic rejection of Dirk's proven approach? Will you fall in love with a new full-time hobby like stamp collecting or hopscotch? If this is your fate, then have fun spending oh-such-precious-time with your infant children and doting wife, progressing up your company's career ladder, and finally getting around to planting that rose garden. Enjoy family vacations in Martha's Vineyard, weekly squash games at the local racquet club, and reading the morning paper—the *financial* section, for God's sake—over a bowl of toasted oats and skim milk. After tasting fantasy victory's sweet nectar, you have elected to walk away, thus wasting my time and yours. You sicken me.

Or was this journey worthwhile? Will you fully incorporate my counsel into your daily fantasy routine? And even more importantly, will you build upon my findings, thereby expanding your knowledge and evolving into the next heralded fantasy star—one who shines even brighter than yours truly? Then yes, these days or weeks or (if you are a "careful" reader) months we have spent together were meaningful after all. You are no longer a Jo-Jo. You are "what *will* be." With opened eyes, a receptive brain, and a willing temperament, you hold the promise of a can't-miss college kid destined for NFL immortality. You learned how to play the *right* way from a coach and mentor who demonstrated how hard work, discipline, and an unyielding desire to continue learning will transform you into a legendary competitor, to be feared and admired by all who dare to challenge you.

The pit of mediocrity is deep and slippery, my friend, and is almost inescapable. Most fantasy competitors wallow in such loser holes their whole lives, oblivious to what lies beyond. I have offered my hand to usher you into the daylight. As a result, your fantasy world view is no longer limited, but boundless, stretching beyond what once was inconceivable. The lowest depths lay behind you. Before you, the highest summit awaits. Very few have seen it. Fewer still have the tools to climb it. You possess everything required to continue your journey to fantasological enlightenment.

During this next and final phase of your life, remember that you cannot spell "fantasological" without "logical." May logic be your guide through the rocky terrain of imperfection. May your research be forever diligent, your emotions forever restrained, and your picks forever justifiable. May your dedication never waver, nor your competitive spirit wane.

May you reach the mountaintop, and desire nothing more in life than to remain there, amidst fellow winners who dare to flourish in a world powerless to hold us back.

Now go kick ass, Dirk.

Fantasy Questions?

If you enjoyed *Fantasy Football for Winners* and would like more customized insights on how to improve your fantasy team, email the author at bjrudell@gmail.com. He will be happy to offer advice on any sport, provided you promise to donate half of your league winnings to a charity of your choice.

Other Books by the Author:

Only in New Hampshire: My Journey on the Campaign Trail

Follow the Author on:

Twitter: twitter.com/bjrudell

Scan the QR code below to visit the author's website:

About the Illustrator

Will Harding is an award-winning designer born and raised in Washington, DC. He is proud to have worked with clients ranging from well-known startups to Fortune 500 brands. He also is a fine artist who has shown locally and continues to pursue his goals as a painter.

When not drawing or designing, Will is avidly searching for the best ways to win his hometown fantasy football league, aptly named The Degenerates, without drafting any players from the Redskins' rivals. A graduate of Syracuse University (2003 National Champions), he later moved back to Washington, DC, where he now resides with his lovely wife, Amanda.

Additional Books from Extra Point Press

Fantasy Football Guidebook: Your Comprehensive Guide to Playing Fantasy Football

-Named one of the Top 4 Fantasy Football books of All-Time by RotoNation.com

-Award-winning finalist in the Sports category of the National Best Books 2008 Awards, sponsored by USA Book News

-Finalist in the Sports category of the 2009 National Indie Excellence Awards

Fantasy Football Tips: 201 Ways to Win through Player Rankings, Cheat Sheets and Better Drafting

Fantasy Football Tips has become an even bigger hit than *Fantasy Football Guidebook*, beating the one-year sales mark in only nine months of availability!

Fantasy Football Basics: The Ultimate "How-to" Guide for Beginners

Fantasy Football Almanac: The Essential Fantasy Football Reference Guide

Fantasy Baseball for Beginners

Fantasy Soccer: The Ultimate "How-to" Guide for Fantasy Soccer Players

Fantasy Hockey: The Ultimate "How-to" Guide for Fantasy Hockey Players

Fantasy Basketball Handbook: The Ultimate "How-to" Guide for Beginner and Experienced Players

CPSIA information can be obtained at www.ICGtesting.com
Printed in the USA
BVOW03s1925181214

380065BV00021B/952/P